POTENTIAL BARRIERS
IN SEMICONDUCTORS

ACADEMIC PAPERBACKS*

BIOLOGY

Edited by ALVIN NASON

Design and Function at the Threshold of Life: The Viruses
HEINZ FRAENKEL-CONRAT
Time, Cells, and Aging BERNARD L. STREHLER
Isotopes in Biology GEORGE WOLF
Life: Its Nature, Origin, and Development A. I. OPARIN

MATHEMATICS

Edited by W. MAGNUS and A. SHENITZER

Finite Permutation Groups HELMUT WIELANDT
Introduction to p-Adic Numbers and Valuation Theory
GEORGE BACHMAN
Quadratic Forms and Matrices N. V. YEFIMOV
Elements of Abstract Harmonic Analysis
GEORGE BACHMAN
Noneuclidean Geometry HERBERT MESCHKOWSKI

PHYSICS

Edited by D. ALLAN BROMLEY

Elementary Dynamics of Particles H. W. HARKNESS
Elementary Plane Rigid Dynamics H. W. HARKNESS
Crystals: Their Role in Nature and in Science CHARLES BUNN
Potential Barriers in Semiconductors B. R. GOSSICK
Mössbauer Effect: Principles and Applications
GUNTHER K. WERTHEIM

* Most of these volumes are also available in a cloth bound
edition.

POTENTIAL BARRIERS
IN SEMICONDUCTORS

by

B. R. GOSSICK

Harpur College
State University of New York
Binghamton, New York

ACADEMIC PRESS   NEW YORK AND LONDON

ACADEMIC PRESS INC.
111 Fifth Avenuc, New York, New York 10003

United Kingdom Edition published by
ACADEMIC PRESS INC. (LONDON) LTD.
Berkeley Square House, London W.1

LIBRARY OF CONGRESS CATALOG CARD NUMBER: 64–24658

PRINTED IN THE UNITED STATES OF AMERICA

POTENTIAL BARRIERS IN SEMICONDUCTORS

BY B. R. R. GOSSICK

ERRATA

Page	Place:	For:	Read:
43	Line 8 from bottom	(111.1)	S/κ
48	Rewrite Equation (113.3) as follows:		
	$$\tau \int \int_g \frac{\partial E}{\partial p_1} \frac{\partial f_0}{\partial p_1} \, dg = \frac{2\theta_n \tau}{h^3} \int_{-p_2\max}^{p_2\max} \int_{-p_3\max}^{p_3\max} \underbrace{\frac{\partial E}{\partial p_1} f_0 \Big|_{-p_1\max}^{p_1\max}}_{\text{vanishes}} dp_2 \, dp_3 - \tau \int \int_g f_0 \frac{\partial^2 E}{\partial p_1^2} \, dg$$		
65	Equation (125.7)	$p(x)$	$p_1(x)$
65	Line 2 following Equation (125.9)	$\varphi_n(x)$	$\varphi_p(x)$
83	Equation (212.1)	$-x_p \ll x < 0$	$-x_p < x < 0$
101	Equation (301.3)	$n \exp[\,\cdot\,]$	$n_i \exp[\,\cdot\,]$
111	Equations (302.12), (302.13) }	$\operatorname{erf} q \dfrac{(V_B - V)}{\kappa T}$	$\operatorname{erf}\left[q \dfrac{(V_B - V)}{\kappa T} \right]^{1/2}$
112	Equation (302.14)	L_p	$L_p{}'$
121	Equation (312.5)	$J'(t)$	$I'(t)$
122	Equation (312.8)	majority	both
123	Equation (312.10)	π	τ
123	Figure 31.3		

POTENTIAL BARRIERS IN SEMICONDUCTORS

BY B. R. GOSSICK

ERRATA

Page	Place:	For:	Read:
5	Line 3 from bottom	(101.7)	(101.9)
5	Last line	continuous	dotted˙
16	Line 7 from bottom	$1 = \ldots$	$l = \ldots$
16	Lines 5 and 6 from bottom	Delete: adding a constant term $(\zeta_i/2)$	$-2E_a$ to the energy E,
23	Equation (101.49)	$z = 0$	$z = \pm 1, \pm 3, \pm 5, \ldots$
24	Lines 2 and 3	with $a = 2$ Å, we have $\Delta = 0.038$ eV and $(k_i)^{-1} = 14$ Å.	if we take $a = 3.5$ Å, $\zeta_i = 1$ eV, $\Delta = 0.038$ eV, then we have $k_i^{-1} \sim 20$ Å.
30	Equation (102.15)	n^2	n_i^2
31	Equation (102.20)	$\dfrac{\theta_n N_c}{2}$	$\dfrac{N_c}{2}$
32	Equation (102.25)	$\dfrac{\theta_p N_v}{2}$	$\dfrac{N_v}{2}$
33	Exercise	$\ln \sqrt{\dfrac{N_v}{N_c}}$	$\kappa T \ln \sqrt{\dfrac{N_v}{N_c}}$

To K. Lark-Horovitz,

a pioneer in semiconductor physics

PREFACE

A potential barrier is the key mechanism which dominates the electrical behavior of many semiconducting systems extending from electronic devices to disordered regions produced by fast neutrons. It follows as a natural consequence that the importance of the physical processes related to potential barriers in semiconductors is now recognized in the curricula of physics, electrical engineering, engineering science, and metallurgy. To discuss these processes, the following topics are relevant: energy bands, charge transport, variations in the electrochemical potentials under nonequilibrium conditions, and the current by electrons and holes associated with fluctuations in a potential barrier. The purpose of this monograph is to introduce these topics to advanced undergraduate and first-year graduate students of engineering, physics, and chemistry. It should also serve as a reference for the following subjects which have been rarely discussed in texts: nonequilibrium carrier statistics, the Dember effect, the Bethe model of a barrier, the injection of hot carriers into a metal from a semiconductor, and the transient behavior of rectifying contacts

The phrase "potential barrier at the boundary surface between two different media" applies also to the chemical processes of corrosion, colloid chemistry, and the function of membranes in biological systems. As the workers in those different fields discuss potential barriers with different terminology, the intercommunication is restricted. Although the examples of potential barriers presented here include only semiconductors and metals, there has been an effort to discuss potential barriers from a general point of view with a simplicity that would facilitate application by workers in the fields of chemistry and biology.

Thus, the over-all objective has been to provide a concise presentation of certain principles which apply to the physical properties of potential barriers in semiconductor rectifiers, transistors, integrated circuitry, surface chemistry, and biology. In striving for this objective, the historical development has been neglected. Pertinent references are cited for those readers who want to study further.

The emphasis in the introductory material has been placed on energy bands and nonequilibrium statistical mechanics. Both topics are important in the theory of potential barriers. Furthermore, the treatments of both topics are not commonly available as given here. The one-electron Schroedinger difference equations have been presented as didactic exercises to illustrate the basic properties of band theory without confronting the formal complexities of more accurate methods. Rather than the customary *ad hoc* introduction of the quasi-Fermi level in the nonequilibrium statistical mechanics, it is instead established by an argument after Brillouin (1934).

All equations have been written in the mks (meter-kilogram-second) system of units. However, some numerical examples have been given in other units, the choice being dictated by common usage.

I am pleased to acknowledge that several of the methods of presenting theories and physical models have been obtained from discussions in years past with scientists in the physics department of Purdue University, and the Solid State Division of Oak Ridge National Laboratory. Appreciation is expressed in particular to Messers F. English, H. K. Henisch, R. Rutherford, and C. Zimmer for comments, and to Mrs. L. Hawker and Mrs. P. Allie for typing the manuscript.

B. R. GOSSICK

CONTENTS

CHAPTER 1

A Review of
the Properties of
Electrons in Crystals

1.0. Conduction Electrons and Holes in Equilibrium

A brief review of electron energy bands is given first. The main features are covered in a detailed treatment in Section 1.0.1, which may be skipped by those readers to whom all points in the review are clear.

To a fairly good approximation, the energy and momentum of a valence electron in a crystal are determined by the solution of a one-electron Hamiltonian. The statement of the one-dimensional Hamiltonian is sketched in Fig. 10.1a, b† in which the Hartree lattice potential is indicated by $\zeta_i(x)$, a function of the coordinate x. The solution, showing the eigenvalues of energy $E(\mathbf{p})$ as a function of momentum in the x direction p_x, is sketched in Fig. 10.1b. The total energy E, the sum of the kinetic energy $|\mathbf{p}|^2/2m^*$, and potential energy $-q\zeta_i$, measured from two arbitrarily chosen reference points (Fig. 10.1a) falls between the limits $E_{\max}$ and $E_{\min}$ indicated by the eigenvalue solution sketched in Fig. 10.1b. The eigenvalue solutions of $E(\mathbf{p})$ periodically repeat in $\mathbf{p}$ space, and the region about the origin, enclosing a period is called the reduced zone, or the first Brillouin zone (Fig. 10.1b).

Of course, the energy $E(\mathbf{p})$ is not a continuous function, but consists of closely spaced discrete levels, the number of levels in a band being of the order of the number of valence electrons in the crystal. As the levels are so closely spaced and so numerous, and as the occupancy of levels in a semi-

---

† Figures are numbered consecutively within each section. The number to the left of the decimal point is the section number; the number to the right of the decimal point is the figure number.

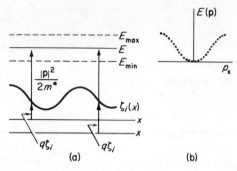

FIG. 10.1. (a) The one-electron Hamiltonian. (b) Eigenvalues of
energy plotted in momentum space.

conductor is so small compared with the number of levels,
the electrons (or holes) may make transitions almost freely
over the energy band, and by such small increments that the
carriers behave almost as though they were free. Furthermore,
the electrons in a semiconductor collect around an energy
minimum in **p** space (holes around a maximum), and, as a
consequence, occupy a region in which energy is quadratic
in momentum. Therefore, the dependence of energy on momentum of electrons and holes closely resembles that of free
particles. Electrons and holes in a semiconductor respond to
applied forces and behave statistically very much like free
particles, and the extent to which the individual characteristics of the periodic potential of the crystal $\zeta_i(x)$ enters is
accounted for by modifying the electronic mass m to an
effective mass m^*. This method of treating electrons and
holes is referred to as the *free electron model*. In a three-
dimensional problem, it turns out that $(m^*)^{-1}$ becomes a
second rank tensor in the manner that the moment of inertia
becomes a second rank tensor in classical mechanics.

Electron energy bands in crystals have been treated ex-
tensively (Herman, 1958; Wannier, 1959), as have the discrete states localized around a lattice imperfection (James,
1949; Slater, 1949).

1.0.1. Electron Energy Bands

As is well known, electrons are the links in the chemical bond, and it follows that the crystal structure, strength and color of solids, the transfer of heat and electric charge in metals, are all governed by the electron density. Therefore, the electronic wave function ψ, whose squared amplitude $|\psi|^2$ gives the electron density, is the key to many physical properties of solids; i.e., the wave function for a valence (outer shell) electron. In rough approximation, we might expect that the electronic wave function ψ, in a solid, might be about the same throughout an atom whether or not it is bound in a solid. Those variations in ψ, which are characteristic of a solid, must occur chiefly in the peripheral parts of the atoms. In point of fact, we have just summarized the argument for the *tight binding approximation*, which employs perturbation theory to obtain the solution of a one-electron Schroedinger equation† of a crystalline array of atoms from the Hartree potential† and wave functions of the free atom of the same species. We now present a one-electron Schroedinger difference equation for a solid as an alternative to the tight binding approximation, which yields similar results, but has an advantage in simplicity of form and interpretation.

1.0.1.1. One-Dimensional Lattice

We commence with a one-dimensional case, making use of the schematic illustration of a one-dimensional crystal, with lattice spacing a, shown in Fig. 10.2. The spatial coordinate x cannot vary continuously, but is restricted to integral

---

† The treatment of a many-electron system by a one-electron Schroedinger equation, as an approximation in which each electron moves in a static potential, is due to Hartree. The interactions of the given electron with all the other electrons, and with all the nuclei, are approximately accounted for by making a suitable choice of the static potential function which is called the Hartree potential. The Hartree potential in a crystalline solid, which, of course, is periodic with the periodicity of the crystal lattice, has been discussed by Wannier (1959).

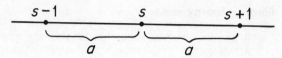

FIG. 10.2. A one-dimensional crystal with lattice spacing a.

values, $x = sa$, $s = 0$, ± 1, ± 2, ± 3, ... In other words, each permissible value of x is associated with the location of a given atom. It is assumed that, for each value of $x = sa$, the electronic wave function $\psi(x) = \psi_s$, may be represented by a typical value, averaged over a suitable region surrounding the point $x = sa$. This being the case, the Schroedinger differential equation,

$$-\frac{\hbar^2}{2m}\frac{d^2\psi(x)}{dx^2} + \zeta_i(x)\psi(x) = E\psi(x) \qquad (101.1)\dagger$$

may be replaced by the corresponding difference equation‡

$$-\frac{\hbar^2}{2m}\left(\frac{\psi_{s+1} + \psi_{s-1} - 2\psi_s}{a^2}\right) + \zeta_{is}\psi_s = E\psi_s \qquad (101.2)$$

which must hold for every location in the crystal as specified by $s = 0$, ± 1, ± 2, ± 3, ... We take a perfect crystal, so that the value of the potential ζ_{is} must be the same at all locations specified by s, and we may as well let $\zeta_{is} = 0$. Hence, (101.2) reduces to the expression

$$\psi_{s+1} + \psi_{s-1} - 2\psi_s + \left(\frac{a}{r_B}\right)^2\frac{E}{E_R}\psi_s = 0 \qquad (101.3)$$

in which r_B is the Bohr radius 0.529 Å, and E_R the Rydberg, 13.6 eV. We use Born–Karman conditions making $\psi_s = \psi_{s+N}$, with N a very large even number, so that the solution applies

---

† Equations are numbered consecutively within each subsection. The number to the left of the decimal point is the subsection number; the number to the right of the decimal point is the equation number.

‡ A method for obtaining the difference equation approximation for the Laplacian is given in Appendix C.

only to the crystal type and not to the boundary conditions of a particular example. Hence, having adopted Born–Karman conditions, making ψ_s periodic, we may write

$$\psi_s = \sum_k C_k e^{iksa} \qquad (101.4)$$

with wave vectors

$$k = \frac{2\pi l}{Na}, \qquad l = 0, \pm 1, \pm 2, \ldots \qquad (101.5)$$

which are harmonics of the fundamental $2\pi(Na)^{-1}$. Now substitute (101.4) into (101.3), multiply through by $\exp(-ik'sa)$ in which k' also satisfies (101.5), and sum over s from $-N/2$ to $+N/2$, which steps are contained in the expression

$$\sum_{s=-N/2}^{s=+N/2} \sum_k C_k \left\{ e^{ika} + e^{-ika} - \left[2 - \left(\frac{a}{r_B} \right)^2 \frac{E}{E_R} \right] \right\}$$

$$\times \exp[i(k - k')sa] = 0 \quad (101.6)$$

According to the *random phase approximation* of Bohm and Pines (1952, 1953) (101.6) reduces to the relation

$$e^{ik'a} + e^{-ik'a} - \left[2 - \left(\frac{a}{r_B} \right)^2 \frac{E}{E_R} \right] = 0 \qquad (101.7)$$

We have, from (101.7), replacing k' by k

$$E(k) = E_w \left(\sin \frac{ka}{2} \right)^2 \qquad (101.8)$$

with

$$E_w = \left(\frac{2r_B}{a} \right)^2 E_R \qquad (101.9)$$

for the eigenvalue $E(k)$ corresponding to each k. Taking $a = 2$ Å, relation (101.7) indicates that $E_w = 3.8$ eV is a typical width of an energy band. The electron energy $E(k)$, which is plotted in Fig. 10.1b as a continuous curve in the reduced zone, $-\pi/a < k < \pi/a$, is limited to $N + 1$ discrete levels within the range $0 < E < E_w$ and with the following spacing between levels:

$$\Delta E = \frac{\pi E_w}{N} \sin \frac{2\pi l}{N}, \qquad -\frac{N}{2} < l < \frac{N}{2} \quad (101.10)$$

while the allowed wave vectors are separated by a constant spacing

$$\Delta k = \frac{2\pi}{Na} \qquad (101.11)$$

As N is such a large number, $\Delta E/\Delta k$, with Δk given by (101.11), may be regarded as equivalent to the limit

$$\frac{dE}{dk} = \lim_{\Delta k \to 0} \frac{\Delta E}{\Delta k} = \frac{Na\Delta E}{2\pi} \qquad (101.12)$$

Hence, we may write for the electron velocity

$$v(k) = \hbar^{-1} \frac{dE}{dk} = \frac{\hbar}{ma} \sin ka \qquad (101.13)$$

or

$$v(k) = \frac{r_B \alpha c_l}{a} \sin ka \qquad (101.14)$$

with α the fine structure constant $(137)^{-1}$ and c_l the velocity of light in vacuum. Therefore, for the effective mass, we have

$$(m^*)^{-1} = \hbar^{-2} \frac{d^2 E}{dk^2} = \frac{\cos ka}{m} \qquad (101.15)$$

in which it is assumed that N is so large as to justify taking the derivative of (101.14). Nondegenerate semiconductors are characterized by an electron energy band which is almost unoccupied, with a small population of occupied states at a minimum of the energy band, and therefore the effective mass of the conduction electrons is positive. On the other hand, nondegenerate semiconductors also have an electron energy band which is almost completely occupied, with a small population of unoccupied states at a maximum of the energy band, where the effective mass is negative. Accordingly, with the simple example (101.15), the effective mass at the bottom of the band is m and at the top $-m$.

We digress to make a point concerning the approximation of (101.1) by (101.2), and begin by remarking that (101.5) is quite general. As the potential $\zeta_i(x)$ in (101.1) is periodic in the crystal lattice, $\zeta_i(x) = \zeta_i(x + ja)$, $j = \pm 1, \pm 2, \pm 3, \ldots$, then (101.1) is Hill's equation, and therefore by Floquet's theorem the solution is the Bloch function $\psi(x) = [\exp(ikx)]y(x)$ with $y(x) = y(x + ja)$. Hence, through Born–Karman conditions we have (101.5); which together with the uncertainty relation makes a the minimum discernible variation in the spatial coordinate x when the wave vector k is confined to the reduced zone $(-\pi/a \leq k \leq \pi/a)$. On the basis of that argument, the spatial coordinate x may be restricted to integral values $x = sa$, making (101.2) approximate (101.1) to the same degree as the tight binding approximation. On the other hand, the weakness of the approximation is that it provides no information about the electron density, $|\psi_s|^2$ being a constant for every coordinate in the crystal. We now consider the requirements for taking into account the variations of electron density within the crystal.

The electron density given by (101.1) may be generally written $|\psi(x)|^2 = |y(x)|^2$ on the basis of Floquet's theorem. Thus, the electron density is periodic with period a rather than Na, so that the electron density may be expressed by the expansion

$$|\psi(x)|^2 = \sum_k D_k \exp(ikx) \qquad (101.15a)$$

with $k = 2\pi z/a$, $z = 0, \pm 1, \pm 2, \pm 3, \ldots$. Suppose that the electron density may be adequately represented by breaking off the series (101.15a) at $k = \pm 10\pi/a$, i.e., $|z|_{max} = 5$, then the maximum variation in the wave vector is $(\Delta k)_{max} = 20\pi/a$ making the minimum discernible variation in the

spatial coordinate $a/10$, by the uncertainty relation. Therefore, to approximate (101.1) by difference equations in
sufficient detail to provide the electron density (101.15a),
expanded out to $z = \pm 5$, it would be necessary to replace
the single equation (101.2) by ten simultaneous equations.

1.0.1.2. Three-Dimensional Lattice

Let us generalize the difference equation method from one
to three dimensions. Take the body-centered cubic lattice;
the following Cartesian coordinates and wave functions apply
to the s atom and its nearest neighbors:

$$\mathbf{r}_{s0} = (s_1, s_2, s_3), \qquad\qquad \psi_{s0}$$

$$\mathbf{r}_{s1} = \left(s_1 + \frac{a}{2}, s_2 + \frac{a}{2}, s_3 + \frac{a}{2}\right), \qquad \psi_{s1}$$

$$\mathbf{r}_{s2} = \left(s_1 - \frac{a}{2}, s_2 + \frac{a}{2}, s_3 + \frac{a}{2}\right), \qquad \psi_{s2}$$

$$\mathbf{r}_{s3} = \left(s_1 - \frac{a}{2}, s_2 + \frac{a}{2}, s_3 - \frac{a}{2}\right), \qquad \psi_{s3}$$

$$\mathbf{r}_{s4} = \left(s_1 + \frac{a}{2}, s_2 + \frac{a}{2}, s_3 - \frac{a}{2}\right), \qquad \psi_{s4}$$

$$\mathbf{r}_{s5} = \left(s_1 + \frac{a}{2}, s_2 - \frac{a}{2}, s_3 + \frac{a}{2}\right), \qquad \psi_{s5}$$

$$\mathbf{r}_{s6} = \left(s_1 - \frac{a}{2}, s_2 - \frac{a}{2}, s_3 + \frac{a}{2}\right), \qquad \psi_{s6}$$

$$\mathbf{r}_{s7} = \left(s_1 - \frac{a}{2}, s_2 - \frac{a}{2}, s_3 - \frac{a}{2}\right), \qquad \psi_{s7}$$

$$\mathbf{r}_{s8} = \left(s_1 + \frac{a}{2}, s_2 - \frac{a}{2}, s_3 - \frac{a}{2}\right), \qquad \psi_{s8}$$

With the body-centered cubic lattice, the difference form of the Laplacian, at the s atom, may be written

$$(\nabla^2 \psi)_{s0} = \frac{1}{a^2}\left\{\sum_{i=1}^{8}\psi_{si} - 8\psi_{s0}\right\} \qquad (101.16)$$

As in the one-dimensional case, we consider a perfect bcc crystal and assign to each coordinate in the system a potential of zero. Hence, the difference form of the one-electron Schroedinger equation for the bcc lattice may be written, from (101.16),

$$\sum_{i=1}^{8}\psi_{si} - 8\psi_{s0} + \left(\frac{a}{r_B}\right)^2 \frac{E}{E_R}\psi_{s0} = 0 \qquad (101.17)$$

Born–Karman conditions are applied by assuming ψ to be periodic with period Na along each of three Cartesian axes defined by the axes of the cubic lattice, N being, again, a very large even number. It is assumed that the solution takes the following form:

$$\psi_{si} = \sum_{k} C_k \exp(i\mathbf{k}\cdot\mathbf{r}_{si}) \qquad (101.18)$$

with the wave vectors satisfying the following relations:

$$\mathbf{k} = (l_1, l_2, l_3)\frac{2\pi}{Na} \qquad (101.19)$$

$$\mathbf{k} = (k_1, k_2, k_3) \qquad (101.20)$$

The l's in (101.19) are integers and each spans the range $-N/2$ to $+N/2$ in the reduced zone. Now substitute (101.18) into (101.17), and multiply through by $\exp(-i\mathbf{k}'\cdot\mathbf{r}_{s0})$, in which $\mathbf{k}'$ also satisfies (101.19) and (101.20). Then sum over all atoms in a cube with length Na per side with the s atom located in the center. Then, using the random phase approximation, we have

$$\exp[i(k_1 + k_2 + k_3)a/2] + \exp[i(-k_1 + k_2 + k_3)a/2]$$
$$+ \exp[i(k_1 + k_2 - k_3)a/2] + \exp[i(k_1 - k_2 + k_3)a/2]$$
$$+ \exp[-i(k_1 + k_2 + k_3)a/2$$
$$+ \exp[-i(-k_1 + k_2 + k_3)a/2]$$
$$+ \exp[-i(k_1 + k_2 - k_3)a/2]$$
$$+ \exp[-i(k_1 - k_2 + k_3)a/2] - \left[8 - \left(\frac{a}{r_B}\right)^2 \frac{E}{E_R}\right] = 0$$

$$(101.21)$$

By trigonometric manipulation (101.21) may be reduced to the following expression for the eigenvalues $E(\mathbf{k})$:

$$E(\mathbf{k}) = 8\left(\frac{r_B}{a}\right)^2 E_R\left(1 - \cos\frac{k_1 a}{2}\cos\frac{k_2 a}{2}\cos\frac{k_3 a}{2}\right) \quad (101.22)$$

Taking $a = 4.3$ Å, relation (101.22) indicates that 3.3 eV is a typical width of the energy band.

As N is very large, we may take the gradient of (101.22) to obtain the velocity

$$\begin{pmatrix} v_1 \\ v_2 \\ v_3 \end{pmatrix} = \frac{2r_B\alpha c_l}{a} \begin{pmatrix} \sin\dfrac{k_1 a}{2}\cos\dfrac{k_2 a}{2}\cos\dfrac{k_3 a}{2} \\[2ex] \cos\dfrac{k_1 a}{2}\sin\dfrac{k_2 a}{2}\cos\dfrac{k_3 a}{2} \\[2ex] \cos\dfrac{k_1 a}{2}\cos\dfrac{k_2 a}{2}\sin\dfrac{k_3 a}{2} \end{pmatrix} \quad (101.23)$$

and the second partial derivatives of (101.22) to obtain the

$(m^*)^{-1}$ tensor

$$\left(\frac{m}{m^*}\right)_{11} = \left(\frac{m}{m^*}\right)_{22} = \left(\frac{m}{m^*}\right)_{33} = \cos\frac{k_1 a}{2}\cos\frac{k_2 a}{2}\cos\frac{k_3 a}{2}$$

(101.24)

$$\left(\frac{m}{m^*}\right)_{12} = \left(\frac{m}{m^*}\right)_{21} = \sin\frac{k_1 a}{2}\sin\frac{k_2 a}{2}\cos\frac{k_3 a}{2}$$

(101.25)

$$\left(\frac{m}{m^*}\right)_{13} = \left(\frac{m}{m^*}\right)_{31} = \sin\frac{k_1 a}{2}\cos\frac{k_2 a}{2}\sin\frac{k_3 a}{2}$$

(101.26)

$$\left(\frac{m}{m^*}\right)_{23} = \left(\frac{m}{m^*}\right)_{32} = \cos\frac{k_1 a}{2}\sin\frac{k_2 a}{2}\sin\frac{k_3 a}{2}$$

(101.27)

It has been pointed out (Section 1.0.1.1) that our difference equations, which try to account for the wave function and potential by recognizing only one location per atom, are too coarse to yield precise results. If it were necessary to account for the electron density in the crystal, recalling that it might be expressed by the Fourier expansion

$$|\psi(\mathbf{r})|^2 = \sum_k C_k \exp(i\mathbf{k}\cdot\mathbf{r}) \tag{101.27a}$$

with $k_j = 2\pi z_j/a$, $z_j = 0$, ± 1, ± 2, ± 3, ... $(j = 1, 2, 3)$ and assuming that an approximation of the electron density would be acceptable with (101.27a) limited to terms up to $z_j = \pm 5$ for each axis ($j = 1, 2, 3$), then the minimum discernible variation in the spatial coordinate along each axis would be $a/10$. Thus, to determine the electron density in this detail, it would be necessary to account for one thousand separate points within a cube of volume a^3, e.g. this would require (101.17) to be replaced by one thousand equations to be solved simultaneously. Difference approximations of wave equations have been discussed by Kron (1945); later we extend the difference approximation to account for two regions per atom in a one-dimensional solution.

The calculations of $E(\mathbf{k})$ given here essentially agree with the tight binding approximation for s states and provide simple exercises in visualizing electron energy levels in wave vector space. Relations (101.22) and (101.23), taken together, illustrate an important feature of the electron velocity $v(\mathbf{k})$ viz., that it is always normal to the surface of equal energy in wave vector space on which $E(\mathbf{k})$ lies.

The difference form of the Laplacian for the face-centered cubic lattice may be written

$$(\nabla^2\psi)_{s0} = \frac{1}{a^2}\left\{\sum_{i=1}^{12}\psi_{si} - 12\psi_{s0}\right\} \qquad (101.28)$$

The coordinates and wave functions for the s atom and its twelve nearest neighbors in the fcc lattice may be designated as follows:

$$\mathbf{r}_{s0} = (s_1, s_2, s_3), \qquad\qquad \psi_{s0}$$

$$\mathbf{r}_{s1} = \left(s_1, s_2 - \frac{a}{2}, s_3 + \frac{a}{2}\right), \qquad \psi_{s1}$$

$$\mathbf{r}_{s2} = \left(s_1, s_2 + \frac{a}{2}, s_3 + \frac{a}{2}\right), \qquad \psi_{s2}$$

$$\mathbf{r}_{s3} = \left(s_1, s_2 - \frac{a}{2}, s_3 - \frac{a}{2}\right), \qquad \psi_{s3}$$

$$\mathbf{r}_{s4} = \left(s_1, s_2 + \frac{a}{2}, s_3 - \frac{a}{2}\right), \qquad \psi_{s4}$$

$$\mathbf{r}_{s5} = \left(s_1 - \frac{a}{2}, s_2 - \frac{a}{2}, s_3\right), \qquad \psi_{s5}$$

$$\mathbf{r}_{s6} = \left(s_1 - \frac{a}{2}, s_2 + \frac{a}{2}, s_3\right), \qquad \psi_{s6}$$

$$\mathbf{r}_{s7} = \left(s_1 + \frac{a}{2}, s_2 - \frac{a}{2}, s_3\right), \qquad \psi_{s7}$$

$$\mathbf{r}_{s8} = \left(s_1 + \frac{a}{2}, s_2 + \frac{a}{2}, s_3\right), \qquad \psi_{s8}$$

$$\mathbf{r}_{s9} = \left(s_1 + \frac{a}{2}, s_2, s_3 + \frac{a}{2}\right), \qquad \psi_{s9}$$

$$\mathbf{r}_{s10} = \left(s_1 - \frac{a}{2}, s_2, s_3 + \frac{a}{2}\right), \qquad \psi_{s10}$$

$$\mathbf{r}_{s11} = \left(s_1 + \frac{a}{2}, s_2, s_3 - \frac{a}{2}\right), \qquad \psi_{s11}$$

$$\mathbf{r}_{s12} = \left(s_1 - \frac{a}{2}, s_2, s_3 - \frac{a}{2}\right), \qquad \psi_{s12}$$

Exercise

Determine the energy levels in the reduced zone of $\mathbf{k}$ space for the fcc lattice, on the basis of the one-electron Schroedinger equation. *Answer*:

$$E(\mathbf{k}) = \frac{\hbar^2}{ma^2}\left[6 - 2\left(\cos\frac{k_1 a}{2}\cos\frac{k_2 a}{2}\right.\right.$$
$$\left.\left. + \cos\frac{k_1 a}{2}\cos\frac{k_3 a}{2} + \cos\frac{k_2 a}{2}\cos\frac{k_3 a}{2}\right)\right]$$

The *diamond lattice* is characterized by two different types of central atom, an s atom and a σ atom, each forming the centroid of a tetrahedron. The difference form of the Laplacian is written the same at either the s or σ atoms, e.g.,

$$(\nabla^2\psi)_{s0} = \frac{8}{a^2}\left\{\sum_{i=1}^{4}\psi_{si} - 4\psi_{s0}\right\} \qquad (101.29)$$

and

$$(\nabla^2\psi)_{\sigma 0} = \frac{8}{a^2}\left\{\sum_{i=1}^{4}\psi_{\sigma i} - 4\psi_{\sigma 0}\right\} \qquad (101.30)$$

The coordinates and wave functions of the s atom and its four nearest neighbors are designated as follows:

$$\mathbf{r}_{s0} = (s_1,\, s_2,\, s_3), \qquad\qquad \psi_{s0}$$

$$\mathbf{r}_{s1} = \left(s_1 - \frac{a}{4},\, s_2 + \frac{a}{4},\, s_3 + \frac{a}{4}\right) \qquad \psi_{s1}$$

$$\mathbf{r}_{s2} = \left(s_1 + \frac{a}{4},\, s_2 + \frac{a}{4},\, s_3 - \frac{a}{4}\right) \qquad \psi_{s2}$$

$$\mathbf{r}_{s3} = \left(s_1 + \frac{a}{4},\, s_2 - \frac{a}{4},\, s_3 + \frac{a}{4}\right) \qquad \psi_{s3}$$

$$\mathbf{r}_{s4} = \left(s_1 - \frac{a}{4},\, s_2 - \frac{a}{4},\, s_3 - \frac{a}{4}\right) \qquad \psi_{s4}$$

The coordinates and wave functions of the σ atom and its four nearest neighbors are designated as follows:

$$\mathbf{r}_{\sigma 0} = (\sigma_1,\, \sigma_2,\, \sigma_3), \qquad\qquad \psi_{\sigma 0}$$

$$\mathbf{r}_{\sigma 1} = \left(\sigma_1 + \frac{a}{4},\, \sigma_2 - \frac{a}{4},\, \sigma_3 - \frac{a}{4}\right) \qquad \psi_{\sigma 1}$$

$$\mathbf{r}_{\sigma 2} = \left(\sigma_1 - \frac{a}{4},\, \sigma_2 - \frac{a}{4},\, \sigma_3 + \frac{a}{4}\right) \qquad \psi_{\sigma 2}$$

$$\mathbf{r}_{\sigma 3} = \left(\sigma_1 - \frac{a}{4},\, \sigma_2 + \frac{a}{4},\, \sigma_3 - \frac{a}{4}\right) \qquad \psi_{\sigma 3}$$

$$\mathbf{r}_{\sigma 4} = \left(\sigma_1 + \frac{a}{4},\, \sigma_2 + \frac{a}{4},\, \sigma_3 + \frac{a}{4}\right) \qquad \psi_{\sigma 4}$$

The difference equation for the one-electron Schroedinger equation for the s and σ atoms may be written, from (101.29) and (101.30),

$$\sum_{i=1}^{4}\psi_{si} - 4\psi_{s0} + \left(\frac{a}{r_B}\right)^2 \frac{E}{8E_R}\psi_{s0} = 0 \qquad (101.31)$$

$$\sum_{i=1}^{4}\psi_{\sigma i} - 4\psi_{\sigma 0} + \left(\frac{a}{r_B}\right)^2 \frac{E}{8E_R}\psi_{\sigma 0} = 0 \qquad (101.32)$$

One proceeds to obtain the solution from (101.31) and (101.32) individually as with the solution for the bcc lattice. After applying the random phase approximation to the two separate expressions obtained from (101.31) and (101.32), one adds them together to obtain a sum similar to (101.21), which yields the following expression for the energy levels in **k** space:

$$E(\mathbf{k}) = \frac{16\hbar^2}{ma^2}\left[1 - \cos\frac{k_1 a}{4}\cos\frac{k_2 a}{4}\cos\frac{k_3 a}{4}\right] \qquad (101.33)$$

Taking $a = 5.4$ Å, (101.33) indicates that 8.4 eV is a typical band width. This may be compared with an estimation, given by Hagstrum (1959), of $\sim$14 eV for the band width of silicon, which has a lattice constant 5.43 Å, and a band width of 7.0 eV (Tomboulian and Bedo, 1956) for germanium which has a lattice constant 5.65 Å. Detailed band calculations have been treated by Brooks (1955) and Herman (1955, 1958), and Callaway (1958, 1964).

1.0.1.3. Valence and Conduction Bands

The discussion returns to the one-dimensional treatment of the one-electron Schroedinger equation, in the difference equation approximation which recognizes two coordinates per atom. The coordinate $x_s = sa$ gives the location of the center of the s atom, and the coordinates $x_{s\pm\frac{1}{2}} = (s \pm \frac{1}{2})a$ designate points midway between the s atom and its nearest neighbors. A perfect lattice is considered, in which the potential is a constant, $-\zeta_i$, at the coordinates sa within the atoms, and zero at the coordinates $(s + \frac{1}{2})a$ between atoms. For this case we have the following two Schroedinger difference equations:

$$\psi_{s+\frac{1}{2}} + \psi_{s-\frac{1}{2}} - 2\psi_s + \frac{\zeta_i + E}{E_a}\psi_s = 0 \qquad (101.34)$$

$$\psi_{s+1} + \psi_s - 2\psi_{s+\frac{1}{2}} + \frac{E}{E_a}\psi_{s+\frac{1}{2}} = 0 \qquad (101.35)$$

with

$$E_a = \left(\frac{2r_B}{a}\right)^2 E_R \qquad (101.36)$$

As before, Born–Karman conditions are applied with a period Na, so that the solution, for the coordinate x_s, may be written

$$\psi_s = \sum_k C_{0k}e^{ikx_s} \qquad (101.37)$$

and, for the coordinate $x_{s+\frac{1}{2}}$,

$$\psi_{s+\frac{1}{2}} = \sum_k C_{\frac{1}{2}k}\exp(ikx_{s+\frac{1}{2}}) \qquad (101.38)$$

in which the wave vector is given by the following relation:

$$k = \frac{2\pi l}{Na} \qquad (101.39)$$

with $1 = 0, \pm1, \pm2, \pm3, \ldots, \pm N/2$ in the reduced zone. For simplicity, we take the option of adding a constant term $(\zeta_i/2) - 2E_a$ to the energy E, replacing $E + (\zeta_i/2) - 2E_a$ by η throughout the remainder of the section. By substituting (101.37) and (101.38), respectively, into (101.34) and (101.35), multiplying through by $\exp(-ik'x_s)$ and $\exp(-ik'x_{s+\frac{1}{2}})$, respectively, summing over all atoms from

$s = -N/2$ to $s = +N/2$, and applying the random phase approximation, one may obtain the following matrix equation:

$$\begin{pmatrix} \left(\dfrac{\eta}{E_a} + \dfrac{\zeta_i}{2E_a}\right) & 2\cos\dfrac{ka}{2} \\ 2\cos\dfrac{ka}{2} & \left(\dfrac{\eta}{E_a} - \dfrac{\zeta_i}{2E_a}\right) \end{pmatrix} \begin{pmatrix} C_{0k} \\ C_{\frac{1}{2}k} \end{pmatrix} = \begin{pmatrix} 0 \\ 0 \end{pmatrix} \qquad (101.40)$$

which has the following eigenvalue solutions:

$$\eta = \pm \sqrt{\left(\frac{\zeta_i}{2}\right)^2 + \left(2E_a \cos\frac{ka}{2}\right)^2} \qquad (101.41)$$

One effect of increasing the number of coordinates from one to two per atom, immediately apparent in (101.41), has been to double the number of electron energy bands. These energy bands are plotted, in the reduced zone, in Fig. 10.3. With semiconductors, the lower energy band is designated as the *valence band* and the upper as the *conduction band*. The separation between bands, the *forbidden gap*, is simply the potential ζ_i, and the relation between the band width E_w

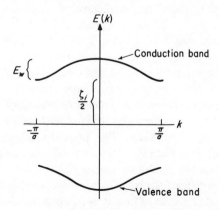

Fig. 10.3. Energy bands given by (101.41) for the reduced zone.

(which is the same for both bands), the potential ζ_i, and the lattice spacing a which enters through the energy parameter $E_a = 2\hbar^2(ma^2)^{-1}$ is indicated by the geometrical construction shown in Fig. 10.4. If the electronic coupling between atoms is loose (E_a small through wide lattice spacing a) and the electrons are tightly bound to the atoms (potential ζ_i is very deep), then it is clear from Fig. 10.4 that the band width E_w must be narrow.

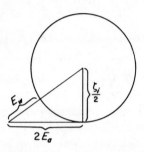

FIG. 10.4. Geometrical construction showing the relation between the band width E_w, potential ζ_i, and energy parameter $E_a = 2\hbar^2(ma^2)^{-1}$.

Taking $a = 2.5$ Å as the nearest neighbor distance, and $\zeta_i = 2.0$ eV as the band gap, relation (101.41) gives 4.0 eV as the band width. The band gaps of some representative semiconductors are listed in Appendix B.

The valence band of a crystal owes its name to the covalent bonds of the crystalline structure, which are formed by the electrons in this band. As practically all of the covalent bonds are complete, the energy states in the valence band are almost all occupied. The configuration of the valence electrons, like any system, favors that with minimum energy at equilibrium. Therefore, the unoccupied states in the valence band lie at the top. These unoccupied states are called *holes*. One has the option of treating the system in terms of either the occupied states (valence electrons) or the unoccupied states (holes), but it is simpler to use the latter for reasons given in Section 1.0.5.

It is convenient to explain some of the salient features of the properties of holes vs. electrons by an analogy based on a sealed bottle containing water and air, in which the total volume of the bottle represents the total number of energy states, the water the occupied states (electrons) and the air the unoccupied states (holes). If the bottle is moving in a gravitational field, the dynamic behavior of the air-water system is more convenient to treat in terms of the water if the bottle is almost full of air, or in terms of the air if the bottle is almost full of water. To compare the two cases, we refer to the water in the first case as a water drop, and the air in the second as an air bubble, and note that, in the same gravitational field, the water drop falls while the air bubble rises. The potential energy of the water drop increases with height and the air bubble with depth. Actually the air bubble behaves like a water drop with negative mass. An analogous force field with the valence electrons is the electric field, in which holes behave like electrons with positive charge. A conclusion of this analogy is that holes may be treated like electrons except that the sign is reversed with energy, charge and mass.

Consider those states at the bottom of the conduction band or the top of the valence band, for which the wave vector may take on the value $\pi/a - k_\delta$ or $-\pi/a + k_\delta$ with $k_\delta \ll \pi/a$. The energy of these states may be expressed by the following quadratic expansions of (101.41):

$$E = \frac{\zeta_i}{2} + \frac{(\hbar k_\delta)^2}{2m^*} \qquad (101.41a)$$

for the conduction band, with

$$\frac{1}{m^*} = \hbar^{-2}\left(\frac{d^2 E}{dk^2}\right)_{k=\pm\pi/a} = \frac{8}{\zeta_i}\left(\frac{\hbar}{ma}\right)^2 \qquad (101.41b)$$

and

$$E = -\frac{\zeta_i}{2} - \frac{(\hbar k_\delta)^2}{2m_h^*} \qquad (101.41c)$$

for the valence band, with

$$\frac{1}{m_h{}^*} = -\hbar^{-2}\left(\frac{d^2E}{dk^2}\right)_{k=\pm\pi/a} = \frac{8}{\zeta_i}\left(\frac{\hbar}{ma}\right)^2 \quad (101.41d)$$

In semiconductors, the states represented by (101.41a) are occupied by electrons, and the states represented by (101.41c) are occupied by holes; while the effective mass of an electron is $\hbar^{-2}\,d^2E/dk^2$, that of a hole is $-\hbar^{-2}\,d^2E/dk^2$ as indicated in (101.41d). The free particle model is illustrated by (101.41a) and (101.41c), e.g., (101.41a) represents the energy of a free electron with mass m^* and wave vector k_δ, while (101.41c) represents the energy of a free hole with mass $m_h{}^*$ and wave vector k_δ.

The ratio $|\,C_{0k}/C_{\frac{1}{2}k}\,|^2$, which may be obtained by inserting (101.41) into (101.40), is of interest because it indicates the relative amount of time spent by an electron in the center of an atom (at an x_s coordinate) as compared with the intermediate position between atoms. We have, for the valence band,

$$\left|\frac{C_{0k}}{C_{\frac{1}{2}k}}\right|^2 = \frac{2\left(\dfrac{\zeta_i}{2}\right)^2 + \left(2E_a \cos\dfrac{ka}{2}\right)^2 + \zeta_i\sqrt{\left(\dfrac{\zeta_i}{2}\right)^2 + 2E_a \cos\left(\dfrac{ka}{2}\right)^2}}{\left(2E_a \cos\dfrac{ka}{2}\right)^2}$$

$$(101.42)$$

which indicates that valence electrons spend more time at the center of atoms than between atoms for all values of k, as $|\,C_{0k}/C_{\frac{1}{2}k}\,|$ always exceeds unity. Furthermore $|\,C_{0k}/C_{\frac{1}{2}k}\,|^2$ increases with increasing $|\,k\,|$, and at the zone boundary $|\,k\,| = \pi/a$, the valence electrons spend all the time at the center of atoms x_s.

With the conduction band, the right side of (101.42) gives the ratio $|\,C_{\frac{1}{2}k}/C_{0k}\,|^2$, so that the conduction electrons spend more time between atoms than at their centers for all values of k; their tendency to favor intermediate sites increases with increasing $|\,k\,|$, to the zone boundary $|\,k\,| = \pi/a$, where they spend all the time at intermediate sites $x_{s+\frac{1}{2}}$.

Ordinarily, each wave vector $\mathbf{k}$ is associated with two electrons of opposite spin. In this case the wave function has only one nonvanishing coefficient C_k in series of the type (101.4), (101.18), (101.37), and (101.38). The energy is given by the eigenvalue solution $E(\mathbf{k})$, and the transport properties include the velocity relation $\hbar^{-1}\nabla_k E$ and the reciprocal effective mass $\hbar^{-2}\,\partial^2 E/\partial k_i \partial k_j$. In order to represent the electron by a wave packet, it is necessary to exercise the full generality of (101.4), (101.18), (101.37), and (101.38). The energy of the wave packet may be written $[\Sigma_k \mid C_k \mid^2 E(\mathbf{k})][\Sigma_k \mid C_k \mid^2]^{-1}$.

The following expression for the electron velocity, based on (101.41a, c) illustrates an important principle, viz., that for a given value of k, the magnitude of velocity is less the narrower the band width:

$$v = \hbar^{-1}\frac{d\eta}{dk} = \mp\frac{2r_B\alpha c}{a}\frac{\sin ka}{\sqrt{\left(\dfrac{\zeta_i}{2E_a}\right)^2 + \left(2\cos\dfrac{ka}{2}\right)^2}} \qquad (101.43)$$

Although (101.43) merely suggests that the mobility (see Sections 1.0.3 and 1.1.3) of an electron in a narrow energy band might be low, the following expression derived from it definitely illustrates that an electron in a narrow band must exhibit a large effective mass:

$$(m^*)^{-1} = \hbar^{-2}\frac{d^2\eta}{dk^2} = \mp\frac{2}{m}\left\{\frac{\cos ka}{\sqrt{\left(\dfrac{\zeta_i}{2E_a}\right)^2 + \left(2\cos\dfrac{ka}{2}\right)^2}}\right.$$
$$\left. + \frac{\sin^2 ka}{\sqrt[3]{\left(\dfrac{\zeta_i}{2E_a}\right)^2 + \left(2\cos\dfrac{ka}{2}\right)^2}}\right\} \qquad (101.44)$$

1.0.1.4. Bound States

Up to now, we have considered only electrons propagating through the lattice, by accounting only for real values of the wave vector k. Take a complex wave vector

$$k = k_r + ik_i \qquad (101.45)$$

The imaginary part of the wave vector, k_i, prevents the electron from propagating through the lattice, and confines it to a particular region. An electron with a complex wave vector occupies a localized energy state, which is outside the

band of energy eigenvalues occupied by electrons with real
wave vectors. Localized electron energy levels in a lattice
arise through the presence of a lattice imperfection (impurity
atom, vacant lattice site, etc.). Such states may contribute
electrons to the conduction band (donor states), extract
electrons from the conduction band (trapping states), serve
as intermediate levels for transitions between the conduction
and valence band (recombination states), or extract electrons
from the valence band creating holes (acceptor states). The
population of these localized energy states in a semiconductor
determines some of its characteristic electronic properties,
e.g., whether the population of conduction electrons predomi-
nates (n type) or holes (p type) (see Section 1.0.2), and the
rate at which excess holes decay through recombination
(see Section 1.2.4). Therefore, many important electronic
properties of semiconductors are associated with electrons
whose wave vectors are complex.

With k complex, as given by (101.45), we may write

$$\left(\sin\frac{ka}{2}\right)^2 = \left(\sin\frac{k_r a}{2}\cosh\frac{k_i a}{2}\right)^2$$

$$- \left(\cos\frac{k_r a}{2}\sinh\frac{k_i a}{2}\right)^2$$

$$+ \frac{i}{2}(\sin k_r a \sinh k_i a) \qquad (101.46)$$

By substituting $1 - (\sin\frac{1}{2}ka)^2$ for $(\cos\frac{1}{2}ka)^2$ in (101.41),
and rearranging, one finds that (101.46) must also satisfy
the relation

$$\left(\sin\frac{ka}{2}\right)^2 = 1 + \left(\frac{\zeta_i}{4E_a}\right)^2 - \left[\frac{\eta(k)}{2E_a}\right]^2 \qquad (101.47)$$

In the range of energy outside the bands, in which electrons
may propagate through the lattice, we let

$$k_r = z\pi/a, \qquad z = 0, \pm 1, \pm 2, \cdots \qquad (101.48)$$

so that $(\sin \tfrac{1}{2}ka)^2$, and, hence, $\eta(k)$ will be real throughout the entire energy range. For localized states within the energy gap between the valence and conduction bands, the wave vector is pure imaginary in the reduced zone,

$$k = ik_i, \qquad z = 0 \qquad (101.49)$$

and (101.46) becomes simply

$$\left(\sin \frac{ka}{2}\right)^2 = 1 + \left(\sinh \frac{k_i a}{2}\right)^2 \qquad (101.50)$$

By substituting (101.50) into (101.47) and rearranging, one may obtain the expression

$$\eta(k) = \pm \sqrt{\left(\frac{\zeta_i}{2}\right)^2 - \left(2E_a \sinh \frac{k_i a}{2}\right)^2} \qquad (101.51)$$

which gives the localized energy states within the forbidden gap, e.g., above the valence band ($-$ sign), and below the conduction band ($+$ sign). The relaxation length $(k_i)^{-1}$ of an electron in a localized state is given by the following relation, which comes from (101.51):

$$\frac{1}{k_i} = a\{\ln\left[\Psi(\eta) + \sqrt{[\Psi(\eta)]^2 - 1}\right\}^{-1} \qquad (101.52)$$

with

$$\Psi(\eta) = 1 + \frac{1}{2}\left(\frac{\zeta_i}{2E_a}\right)^2 - \frac{1}{2}\left(\frac{\eta}{E_a}\right)^2 \qquad (101.53)$$

Equation (101.53) indicates that the relaxation length $(k_i)^{-1}$ increases with decreasing separation between the band edge and the energy of the localized state. Take the case for which the separation $\Delta = (\zeta_i/2) - \eta(k)$, is small compared with either E_a or ζ_i. Then, (101.52) reduces to

$$\frac{1}{k_i} \approx \frac{E_a a}{\sqrt{\zeta_i \Delta}} \qquad (101.54)$$

Taking $\Delta = E_a/100$ and $\zeta_i = 2E_a$, we have $(k_i)^{-1} \approx 7a$ for the relaxation length, and with $a = 2$ Å, we have $\Delta = 0.038$ eV and $(k_i)^{-1} = 14$ Å.

The Schroedinger equation, subject to Born–Karman conditions determines real eigenvalues k with corresponding bands of eigenvalues $E(k)$, but outside these bands the energy is a continuous function of the complex wave vector. Hence, a lattice imperfection may establish a discrete level anywhere within the forbidden energy gap between the valence and conduction bands, and these gaps in both silicon and germanium are populated with a variety of discrete levels. To illustrate how these discrete levels come about, we will consider a donor impurity, substitutionally occupying a normal lattice site. The donor impurity has an extra valence electron not required in the lattice bonds, and it is convenient to regard this impurity with the valence electrons occupying the lattice bonds as a positive ion and the extra electron as a separate entity. In general there is a set of discrete energy levels in which the extra electron may associate with the positive impurity ion. A rough indication of this relationship is given by the *hydrogenic model*, which represents the extra electron and impurity ion by a Bohr hydrogen atom in a continuous medium with relative permittivity $\epsilon > 1$, to account for the screening by the intervening lattice atoms between the extra electron and the impurity ion. In this approximation, we have the localized donor level E_D, separated from the bottom of the conduction band E_c by an amount

$$\Delta_{dn} = -\frac{m^* E_R}{m(n\epsilon)^2} \qquad (101.55)$$

and corresponding Bohr radii

$$r_{dn} = \frac{mn^2\epsilon r_B}{m^*} \qquad (101.56)$$

in which n is the principal quantum number. Taking $\epsilon = 16$, and $(m^*/m) = 0.12$, for germanium, we have a localized level at $\Delta_{d1} = 0.0064$ eV below the conduction band, with a radius $r_{d1} = 70$ Å. It may be seen by applying (101.55) to typical cases, that the separation Δ_{d1} may often not exceed κT at room temperature, and, in some cases, even down to liquid nitrogen temperature. With $\Delta_{d1} < \kappa T$, most of the donor impurities are ionized. Thus, except at very low temperatures, the extra electrons occupy the conduction band rather than the donor levels.

We now illustrate how an acceptor state may extract an electron from the valence band to create a hole. Consider an acceptor impurity substitutionally occupying a normal lattice site. The acceptor impurity lacks a valence electron, but the lattice requirements for filled covalent bonds are so strong that the acceptor impurity has a complete set of bonds part of the time during which it is a negative ion. The missing bond, or hole, moves about the neighborhood of the ionized acceptor by the hydrogenic model. The positive hole is bound to the negative acceptor ion in a localized energy level E_A, separated from the top of the valence band E_v by an amount

$$\Delta_{an} = -\frac{m_h{}^* E_R}{m(n\epsilon)^2} \qquad (101.57)$$

with the corresponding Bohr radius,

$$r_{an} = mn^2\epsilon r_B / m_h{}^* \qquad (101.58)$$

and with n the principal quantum number. If the temperature is sufficient to make $\kappa T > \Delta_{a1}$, then the hole may escape to the valence band and propagate through the crystal as a *free hole*.

If the population of lattice imperfections increases to the point that the mean separation between imperfections is comparable to the relaxation length $(k_i)^{-1}$, or radius r_{d1}, then the electrons are no longer localized, but may propagate from one impurity to the next. Hung (1950) has treated overlapping impurity levels in terms of an *impurity band*. With sufficient impurity density and temperature low enough to populate the impurities, evidence of impurity bands has been observed (Fritzsche and Lark–Horovitz, 1954).

Some characteristics of localized energy states have been illustrated with the difference equation approximation of the Schroedinger equation and the hydrogenic model, each of which is adequate for order of magnitude estimates. For example, the values of Δ_{d1}, and r_{d1} estimated from (101.55) and (101.56) and values of Δ and $(k_i)^{-1}$ from (101.54), for typical values of lattice separation, permittivity, etc., fall in compatible ranges of magnitude. Localized energy levels in crystals have been studied in detail by James (1949) and by Slater (1949). Kohn (1959) has reviewed the theoretical justification for the hydrogenic model and has applied it in a more elegant form.

1.0.2. Dependence of Electron Concentration on Potential and Fermi Level

The study of potential barriers in semiconductors concerns potential fluctuations from inhomogeneities in impurity concentration, variations which appear over distances of a few thousand angstroms. To consider such gross potential fluctuations, we smooth out the Hartree potential (with the periodicity of lattice spacing) and treat it as a slowly varying function of position $\zeta_i(x)$ in the crystal,[†] as shown in Fig. 10.5. The Fermi level ζ, lowest energy of the conduction band E_c, highest energy of the valence band E_v, and total electron energy E are also indicated in Fig. 10.5, which depicts the system with no applied field, and hence no net current. Electrons are undergoing transitions between energy states through thermal collisions with the lattice, but the lattice and electrons are in equilibrium (have the same temperature), and the energy of electrons and phonons is conserved on the average.

[†] The potential $\zeta_i(x)$ is located at the position of the intrinsic Fermi level, approximately midway between the band edges E_v and E_c. See Exercise, p. 33.

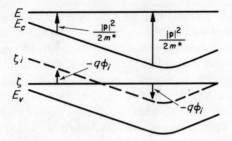

FIG. 10.5. Electron energy band diagram for an inhomogeneous semiconductor in equilibrium.

The establishment of a zero reference of energy for terms such as Fermi level ζ potential energy $\zeta_i = -q\varphi_i$, band edges E_v and E_c, is arbitrary. The intersection of ζ and ζ_i defines the zero energy in Fig. 10.5. In general, the density of electrons in the conduction band may be written

$$n = n_i \exp(\zeta - \zeta_i)/\kappa T \qquad (102.1)$$

or

$$n = N_c \exp(\zeta - E_c)/\kappa T \qquad (102.2)$$

with

$$N_c = 2\theta_n (2\pi m^* \kappa T)^{3/2} h^{-3} \qquad (102.3)$$

$$= 4.82 \cdot 10^{15} \theta_n (m^* T/m)^{3/2} \quad \text{cm}^{-3} \qquad (102.4)$$

The density parameter n_i is the concentration of electrons and holes in intrinsic material (102.15), the density parameter N_c gives the effective density of electrons in the conduction band, and θ_n is the number of energy minima in the reduced zone, as explained later in Section 1.1.2. In N_c, the effective mass is a geometric mean value, obtained by taking the cube root of the mass tensor $\mid m_{ij} \mid^{1/3}$, which equals 0.33 with silicon, and $0.21m$ with germanium. Equations (102.1) and (102.2) are based on the classical approximation of Fermi statistics, and this approximation is valid if n is less than N_c. The concentration of free carriers in a semiconductor is ordinarily less than either N_c or the concentration of atoms in an ideal gas, e.g., N_c equals $2.2 \cdot 10^{19}$ cm^{-3} at 0°C with $\theta_n = 1$ and $m^* = m$, while the density of an ideal gas at 0°C under one atmosphere equals $2.6 \cdot 10^{19}$ cm^{-3}. Therefore, it is not surprising that classical statistics is ordinarily applicable with semiconductors. An easy criterion to remember, for the validity of the classical approximation of Fermi statistics, is the following. If $\langle |\mathbf{p}| \rangle^3$ exceeds nh^3, then the classical approximation applies with the mean momentum $\langle |\mathbf{p}| \rangle$ given by the classical expression $\sqrt{8m^*\kappa T/\pi}$.

In the nondegenerate case, in which the classical approximation of Fermi statistics applies, the density of holes in the valence band is governed by the Fermi level through the following relations, which are entirely analogous to (102.1) to (102.3):

$$p = n_i \exp(\zeta_i - \zeta)/\kappa T \qquad (102.5)$$

or

$$p = N_v \exp(E_v - \zeta)/kT \qquad (102.6)$$

with

$$N_v = 2\theta_p(2\pi m_h^* \kappa T)^{3/2} h^{-3} \qquad (102.7)$$

In (102.7) the parameter N_v gives the effective density of holes in the valence band, m_h^* is the mean effective mass of a hole, and θ_p is the number of energy maxima in the reduced zone.

It has been shown by Fowler (1933) that the density of electrons and holes may be determined from the law of mass action; several examples will be given starting with the intrinsic case. The term *intrinsic* applies to a semiconductor in which the concentrations of electrons in the conduction band and holes in the valence band are effectively equal. In the intrinsic case, the electrons in the conduction band have escaped from the valence band leaving a hole behind, and that is why there is a one to one correspondence between the electrons and holes for the intrinsic case. There are two types of *impurity* semiconductors, viz., n-type and p-type. In an

n-type impurity semiconductor, the electrons in the conduction band have escaped from donor impurity atoms, and in an impurity p-type semiconductor, the holes in the valence band have been created by valence electrons being captured by acceptor impurity atoms. Thus, it is clear that the temperature range over which a semiconductor may exhibit intrinsic behavior has a lower temperature threshold with semiconductors that are relatively pure than with those that are impure.

The dissociation of a valence electron into a hole-electron pair (electron in the conduction band and hole in the valence band), and the recombination of a hole-electron pair to form a valence electron, have fixed rates governed by the temperature within a semiconductor in equilibrium. The equilibrium equation for their reaction may be written

$$n_v \rightleftarrows n + p \qquad (102.8)$$

with n_v the density of electrons in the valence band, p the density of holes in the valence band, n the density of electrons in the conduction band. Let $n_v{}^0$ denote the density of electrons in the valence band at $0°K$. Then we have

$$n_v = n_v{}^0 - p \qquad (102.9)$$

As only the intrinsic case is under discussion, we may write

$$n = p = n_i \qquad (102.10)$$

Furthermore, we restrict the discussion to the nondegenerate case in order to justify using classical statistics, and therefore we may write the following inequality:

$$n_v{}^0 \gg n \qquad (102.11)$$

Denoting $K_1(T)$ for the equilibrium constant, we may write from (102.8) and (102.10)

$$\frac{n_i{}^2}{n_v} = K_1(T) \qquad (102.12)$$

We may rewrite (102.12), taking (102.9) and (102.10) into account:

$$\frac{n_i{}^2}{n_v{}^0 - n_i} = K_1(T) \qquad (102.13)$$

In view of the inequality (102.11), relation (102.13) reduces to

$$n_i{}^2 = n_v{}^0 K_1(T) \qquad (102.14)$$

The equilibrium constant $K_1(T)$ is discussed in a number of reference works on semiconductors (Shockley, 1950; Blakemore, 1962); it is given explicitly in the following expression:

$$n^2 = N_c N_v \exp[-(E_c - E_v)/kT] \qquad (102.15)$$

The strong dependence of the intrinsic carrier concentration n_i on the forbidden gap $(E_c - E_v)$ is illustrated by (102.15). Actually, the forbidden gap distinguishes an insulator from a semiconductor. Suppose there were two substances with the same crystal structure, one with a forbidden gap of 0.5 volt and the other with 5.0 volts. The substance with a gap of 0.5 volt would be a semiconductor, that with a 5.0 volt gap an insulator. The forbidden gaps with germanium and silicon are approximately 0.66 and 1.12 eV, respectively.

Consider the application of the law of mass action to an impurity n-type semiconductor. In this case, the density of electrons in the conduction band depends upon the rate of two processes. In one process, the electrons enter the conduction band by escaping from donor atoms leaving the donors ionized. In the other process, electrons leave the conduction band and are captured by ionized donor impurities making them neutral. The equilibrium equation for these two processes may be written

$$N_D \rightleftarrows n + N_{D+} \qquad (102.16)$$

with N_D the density of neutral donor impurities and N_{D+} the density of ionized donor impurities. The following two relations are inherent in the processes involved in relation (102.16):

$$n = N_{D+} \qquad (102.17)$$

and

$$N_D = N_D{}^0 - n \qquad (102.18)$$

with $N_D{}^0$ the total density of donor impurities. Applying the law of mass action to the equilibrium equation (102.16), taking (102.17) and (102.18) into account, we have

$$\frac{n^2}{N_D{}^0 - n} = K_2(T) \qquad (102.19)$$

The equilibrium constant $K_2(T)$ in (102.19), which is given explicitly in the following relation, may be easily obtained using an extension of Fowler's method by Crawford and Holmes (1954):

$$\frac{n^2}{N_D{}^0 - n} = \frac{\theta_n N_c}{2} \exp\left(\frac{E_D - E_c}{\kappa T}\right) \qquad (102.20)$$

E_D denotes the energy of the donor level, and the difference between E_D and the bottom of the conduction band E_c, i.e. $(E_D - E_c)$ corresponds to (101.55) in the hydrogenic model.

Below the intrinsic temperature range, there is a range of temperature over which most of the donor impurities are ionized, so that the electron concentration is practically constant over this temperature range and approximately equal to the concentration of donor impurities. The term *exhaustion range* is applied to this temperature range, and the term applies also to p-type semiconductors in which most of the acceptor impurities are ionized.

The concentration of holes in the valence band in a p-type semiconductor depends upon the rate of the following processes. Valence electrons are captured by acceptor impurities, creating a hole in the valence band, and, at the same time, ionizing the acceptor impurity. Electrons trapped by ionized impurities escape, and enter the valence band, destroying a hole there, and neutralizing the ionized acceptor impurity. These processes have the following equilibrium equation:

$$N_A \rightleftarrows p + N_{A-} \qquad (102.21)$$

with the N_A density of neutral acceptor impurities and N_{A-} the density of ionized acceptor impurities. It is inherent in the processes involved in (102.21) that the hole concentration must be equal to the concentration of ionized acceptors:

$$p = N_{A-} \qquad (102.22)$$

and that the concentration of neutral acceptor impurities is equal to the concentration of neutral acceptors at $0°K$ minus the hole concentration, e.g.,

$$N_A = N_A{}^0 - p \qquad (102.23)$$

The following expression is a statement of the law of mass action as applied to the equilibrium equation (102.21):

$$\frac{p^2}{N_A{}^0 - p} = K_3(T) \qquad (102.24)$$

Equation (102.24) is rewritten in the following expression with the reaction constant given explicitly:

$$\frac{p^2}{N_A{}^0 - p} = \frac{\theta_p N_v}{2} \exp - \left(\frac{E_A - E_v}{\kappa T} \right) \qquad (102.25)$$

in which the difference between the energy of the top of the valence band E_v, and that of the acceptor level E_A, i.e. $(E_v - E_A)$ is the energy of a hole bound to an acceptor site. In determining the reaction constant in (102.19) and (102.24), using the extension of Fowler's method by Crawford and Holmes (1954), it has been assumed that the extra electron of a neutral donor which is not engaged in lattice bonds is unpaired, and that the extra electron which completes the lattice bond of an ionized acceptor is paired.

The relations between electron and hole concentration, the Fermi level, and energy band edges E_c, and E_A, for nondegenerate and degenerate systems, i.e. semiconductors and metals, respectively, are indicated schematically in Fig. 10.7. The function $g(E)$ represents the number of energy states per unit volume. Its derivative dg/dE is shown and the shading indicates the relative occupancy of the states.

The statement in Section 1.0.1.3 that holes may be treated like electrons except that the sign is reversed with energy, charge, and mass, may now be extended to cover the difference between the Fermi level ζ and potential ζ_i, cf. (102.1), (102.5), the difference between the Fermi level and band edge, cf. (102.2), (102.6), and the difference between an impurity level and band edge, cf. (102.20), (102.25).

Exercise

Show that the Fermi level, in the intrinsic temperature range has the location

$$\zeta_i = \frac{E_v + E_c}{2} + \ln \sqrt{\frac{N_v}{N_c}}$$

which is approximately midway in the forbidden energy gap.

1.0.3. Transport Relations

The transport properties of electrons, briefly reviewed here, are treated in more detail in Sections 1.1.2 and 1.1.3.

The electron velocity $\hbar^{-1}\nabla_k E$ associated with each energy state in the energy band of a perfect lattice has already been considered, (101.13), (101.23). In addition to the velocity $\hbar^{-1}\nabla_k E$, there are superimposed two other contributions in an inhomogeneous lattice, i.e., a lattice with a distribution of imperfections, (1) diffusion velocity through a gradient in electron concentration, and (2) drift velocity produced by an electric field. The velocity contributions by drift and diffusion are treated independently, and accounted for in the total velocity by superposition. Consider the schematic energy band diagram of an inhomogeneous semiconductor indicated in Fig. 10.5. Electrons are directed toward the energy minimum by the electric field $-\nabla\varphi_i$, but, as this is the location of the maximum electron concentration, they are directed away from the energy minimum by diffusion. In equilibrium, there is no net transport of electrons, and this suggests that there should be a characteristic relation balancing the transport by diffusion and by the electric field. There is indeed, and it is the Einstein relation, one of the topics of this section.

The drift current density $\mathbf{J}_1$, for electrons may be written $-qn\langle\mathbf{v}\rangle$ with $\langle\mathbf{v}\rangle$ the mean drift velocity of conduction electrons in the direction opposing the electric field $\mathbf{E}$, averaged over many mean free paths. The drift velocity $\langle\mathbf{v}\rangle$ is linearly related to the electric field, i.e.,

$$\langle\mathbf{v}\rangle = -\mu_n\mathbf{E} \tag{103.1}$$

in which $-\mu_n$ denotes the mobility of electrons in the semiconductor.† Hence, the drift current density may be written

$$\mathbf{J}_1 = (-q)n(-\mu_n)\mathbf{E} = qn\mu_n\mathbf{E} \tag{103.2}$$

In a uniform semiconductor with charge neutrality (no space charge), Ohm's law is obeyed, and there is a conductivity

$$\sigma_n = qn\mu_n = \text{const} \tag{103.3}$$

The diffusion current density of electrons may be written (on the basis of kinetic theory) as

$$\mathbf{J}_2 = (-q)D_n(-\nabla n) = qD_n\nabla n \tag{103.4}$$

The diffusion coefficient D_n, according to kinetic theory, may be written

$$D_n = v_n\lambda_n/3 \tag{103.5}$$

with v_n the mean thermal velocity and λ_n the mean free path of electrons in the semiconductor.

---

† The mobility $-\mu_n$ will be referred to hereafter, in the customary fashion, by its magnitude μ_n.

The total current density **J** summarizes the contributions J_1 by drift, and J_2, by diffusion, e.g.,

$$\mathbf{J} = \mathbf{J}_1 + \mathbf{J}_2 \tag{103.6}$$

The Einstein relation, as mentioned earlier, ensures the cancellation of the diffusion and drift velocities, one by the other, in equilibrium, and as the coefficient D_n and the density gradient $-\nabla n$ give the diffusion velocity, and the coefficient μ_n and the potential gradient $-\nabla\varphi_i$ give the drift velocity, one might expect the Einstein relation to relate the diffusion coefficient D_n to the mobility μ_n. Consider neutral material, with no applied field, material which has local fluctuations in potential, because of inhomogeneities in impurity concentration. As there is no applied field, the current density vanishes according to the statement

$$-qn\mu_n\frac{d\varphi_i}{dx} + qD_n\frac{dn}{dx} = 0 \tag{103.7}$$

$$\frac{dn}{d\phi_i} - \frac{\mu_n n}{D_n} = 0 \tag{103.8}$$

$$n(\varphi_i) = n_0\exp(\mu_n\varphi_i/D_n) \tag{103.9}$$

Taking $\zeta_i = -q\varphi_i$ in (102.1), we may rewrite the Boltzmann relation

$$n(\varphi_i) = n_0\exp(q\varphi_i/\kappa T) \tag{103.10}$$

with

$$n_0 = n_i\exp(\zeta/\kappa T) \tag{103.11}$$

Equating (103.9) and (103.10) gives the Einstein relation

$$\frac{D_n}{\mu_n} = \frac{\kappa T}{q} \tag{103.12}$$

which is required to make the current density vanish as stated by Eq. (103.7). This relation may be verified as follows. By kinetic theory the mobility of an electron in a classical electron gas takes the form

$$\mu_n = \frac{q\tau}{m^*} \qquad (103.13)$$

with τ the collision time of electrons, and m^* the mean effective mass which was discussed in connection with (102.3). The mean kinetic energy per electron may be written in this case as

$$\frac{m^* v_n \lambda_n}{2\tau} = \frac{3\kappa T}{2} \qquad (103.14)$$

which assumes a well-known classical form when λ_n/τ is replaced by v_n. The Einstein relation (103.12) also follows directly from (103.5), (103.13), and (103.14). Some values of carrier mobility (measured at room temperature) for representative semiconductors are listed in Appendix B.

Several points of the Einstein relation are reviewed. An inhomogeneous donor concentration automatically produces an inhomogeneous electron concentration, and the corresponding statement may be made concerning the acceptor and hole concentrations. The special case of particular interest here is the inhomogeneous electron and hole concentrations in potential barriers. With the equilibrium concentration of electrons given by a Boltzmann distribution, (103.10) e.g.,

$$n(x) = n(0) \exp \frac{q}{\kappa T}[\varphi_i(x) - \varphi_i(0)] \qquad (103.15)$$

and the mobility related to the diffusion coefficient by the Einstein relation (103.12), then there can be no net flow of electrons. Furthermore, it follows that, with an equilibrium concentration of holes

$$p(x) = p(0) \exp \frac{q}{\kappa T}[\varphi_i(0) - \varphi_i(x)] \qquad (103.16)$$

and with the mobility and diffusion coefficient of holes conforming to the Einstein relation (103.12), then there can be no net flow of holes.

1.0.4. Impurity Concentration Compatible with Charge Neutrality

We now seek the necessary conditions for inhomogeneous material to be free of space charge. In other words, we consider the conditions imposed on the ionized donor concentration $N_{D+}(x)$ and the ionized acceptor concentration $N_{A-}(x)$ and boundary charge to permit charge neutrality.[†] Consideration is restricted here to the exhaustion temperature range (donor and acceptor impurities are all ionized). Taking the one dimensional case, the charge density may be written

$$\rho(x) = [N_{D+}(x) - N_{A-}(x) + p(x) - n(x)]q \quad (104.1)$$

with

$$p(x) = n_i \exp q(\varphi - \varphi_i)/\kappa T \quad (104.2)$$

the concentration of holes,

$$n(x) = n_i \exp q(\varphi_i - \varphi)/\kappa T \quad (104.3)$$

the concentration of electrons, φ_i, the potential, and $-q\varphi$ the Fermi level. The following expression results from making (104.1) vanish, i.e., making the material neutral:

$$N_{D+}(x) - N_{A-}(x) = 2n_i \sinh q(\varphi_i - \varphi)/\kappa T \quad (104.4)$$

Since the region is neutral, the solution of Poisson's equation gives a potential with linear dependence on distance x, e.g.,

$$\varphi_i(x) = \varphi + (\kappa T/qL_c)x \quad (104.5)$$

in which L_c is a constant characteristic length. Inserting (104.5) into (104.4) yields

$$N_{D+}(x) - N_{A-}(x) = 2n_i \sinh x/L_c \quad (104.6)$$

---

† We consider a region over which the material changes from p- to n-type. As we will learn later, such a region ordinarily is accompanied by a space charge double layer. We conclude in this section that by imposing the neutrality condition on a p-n transition region, we do not really eliminate space charge, but simply separate the two halves of the double layer, making them bound the neutral region.

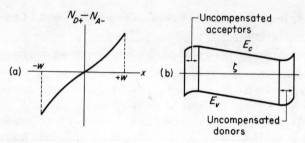

Fig. 10.6. (a) Impurity density, plotted against distance under conditions of neutrality. (b) Electron energy band diagram for the impurity concentration in (a).

The solution (104.6) is sketched in Fig. 10.6a and the energy band structure in Fig. 10.6b.

The impurity distribution $N_{D+}(x) - N_{A-}(x)$ must satisfy (104.6) as a necessary condition for charge neutrality within inhomogeneous material. Although (104.6) is a necessary condition for neutrality it is insufficient, as the boundary conditions for the electric field within the material have yet to be considered. For example, there is a constant field $\kappa T/qL_c$ throughout the neutral region which requires space charge regions at the boundaries (Fig. 10.6b) to satisfy the boundary conditions for an electric field. A conclusion is that over-all neutrality is impossible, and that space charge regions form to satisfy boundary conditions.[†] Space charge layers can form at a boundary also from absorbed impurities, and occupied Tamm (1932) levels. These effects have been described by Bardeen and Morrison (1954).

1.0.5. Summary

(1) Characteristics of a free particle:
   (a) It occupies a region of constant potential, and
   (b) its energy is a continuous (quadratic) function of momentum.

---

† This same problem has been treated by Shockley (1949), but with markedly different conclusions. A general treatment of related problems has been given by Vul and Segal (1958).

(2) Characteristics of an electron in the conduction band, or hole in the valence band:

(a) Either particle lies in a periodic potential, with the period of the lattice spacing, and

(b) its energy is confined to discrete levels bunched together in the conduction band (almost empty) and valence band (almost full) with a forbidden energy gap separating the two bands.

(c) The levels are so closely spaced that the energy is almost a continuous function of momentum. Energy is approximately quadratic in momentum at the bottom of a band (electrons), or top (holes).

(d) If the concentration of electrons (or holes) is so low that the Boltzmann approximation of Fermi statistics applies, electrons are confined to the bottom of the band, (holes to the top) making energy quadratic in momentum and making electrons and holes behave like free particles.

(e) The laws of electromagnetic theory and statistics for free particles are applied, making allowance for crystal lattice forces through replacing the mass by an appropriate effective mass m^*.

The Fermi level ζ is an index of particle concentration, e.g., $(\zeta - E_c)$ for electrons [see (102.2)], and $(\zeta - E_v)$ for holes [see (102.6)]. The distribution in energy of energy states has been sketched schematically for two nondegenerate and two degenerate systems in Fig. 10.7, in which the occupancy of the states has been indicated by shading. The nondegenerate systems have been illustrated by an n-type and p-type semiconductor (Figs. 10.7a and 10.7b) and the degenerate systems by an n-type and p-type metal (Figs. 10.7c and 10.7d). The classical approximation of Fermi–Dirac quantum statistics applies to the nondegenerate systems (Figs. 10.7a and 10.7b), and the distinctive nature of the quantum statistics is brought out in the degenerate systems (Figs. 10.7c and 10.7d).

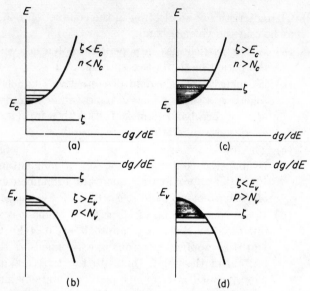

FIG. 10.7. The density of energy states per unit energy versus energy, for (a) electrons in an n-type semiconductor; (b) holes in a p-type semiconductor; (c) electrons in an n-type metal; (d) holes in a p-type metal.

1.1. Nonequilibrium Statistical Mechanics

1.1.1. Statistics of Electrons in Equilibrium

We will briefly review some fundamental concepts of the statistical mechanics which apply to electrons and holes.

Consider a population of conduction electrons as a conservative system, i.e., it is in a stationary state. It follows as a corollary, on the basis of the Hamiltonian canonical equations (by the Liouville theorem) that the density of electrons in six-dimensional phase space is constant. It follows, also, as a corollary, that the number of states in a group s is proportional to the volume occupied by the group in 6-dimensional phase space. The number of energy states per unit volume of three-dimensional x_j ($j = 1, 2, 3$) space, of a group s will be denoted g_s and called the density of states of the s group. This group of states defines a volume in momentum p_j space, and it follows from the second corollary, given above, that g_s is proportional to its volume in momentum space.

Let n_s denote the density of occupied energy states in the s group, and W denote the probability of the system of electrons being in a configuration (g_s, n_s) with s ranging from unity to a very large number. Let S denote the entropy of the system, n the total electron density, u the energy density, and E_s the energy of an electron in the s group. The following three relations form the basis of the statistics of an electronic population in a stationary state:

$$S = \kappa \ln W \qquad (111.1)$$

$$n = \sum_s n_s \qquad (111.2)$$

$$u = \sum_s n_s E_s \qquad (111.3)$$

The system described by (111.1)–(111.3) is in thermodynamic equilibrium, and (111.2) requires that the number of particles be conserved, while (111.3) requires that the energy be conserved. The equilibrium condition (most probable configuration) of the system is determined by maximizing the entropy (111.1) subject to conditions (111.2) and (111.3) using the method of Lagrangian multipliers.

1.1.2. Nonequilibrium Statistical Mechanics

What if we want to study the system in a steady state, in which there is a steady transport of charge, or heat? In the first example there is a conditional equation on the current density of electrons in the x direction,

$$J = -q \sum_s n_s v_{s1} \qquad (112.1)$$

and in the second example, on the electronic contribution to the heat flux in the x direction,

$$\Phi = \frac{m}{2} \sum_s n_s v_s{}^2 v_{s1} \qquad (112.2)$$

and these are both nonconservative relations in conflict with (111.2) and (111.3). Further, the Liouville theorem, which assumes a conservative system, no longer can be used to justify evaluating g_s, the density of states in group s, through its volume in momentum space. However, introduction of either (112.1) or (112.2) need not invalidate (111.1)–(111.3) if they are used subject to an appropriate interpretation. If we evaluate g_s in W, in (111.1), through the uncertainty relation, which is very general and not limited to conservative systems, making g_s in volume $(x_1 x_2 x_3 = 1)$ equal to $2\theta_n \, dp_1 \, dp_2 \, dp_3 \, h^{-3}$ with $2\theta_n$ a degeneracy factor of which the factor 2 accounts for two possible spin orientations and θ_n the number of energy minima† in the "reduced zone" (Blakemore, 1962), then we should be able to treat the entropy of a nonconservative system, provided we suitably define n_s. We meet this problem by defining the space containing all particles as follows: The system at a given time consists of just those particles in the space, although all particles are flowing through the space. Hence, in steady flow, the density of particles in the system is conserved, although the particles are not the same from one instant to the next. As the particles are indistinguishable anyway, this limitation seems unimportant. In the space just defined, the energy density is still given by (111.3), and under conditions of steady flow this energy density is conserved. Hence, the most probable configuration of a system under steady flow of charge, or heat, may be determined by maximizing the entropy (111.1) subject to (111.2), (111.3), and (112.1), or (111.2), respectively.

Alternately g_s may be treated as follows: The one-electron Hamiltonian with a periodic potential appropriate to the

---

† It is assumed here that there is either one minimum at the origin, or that there are an even number of minima symmetrically located about the origin in momentum space, so that only one population of electrons needs to be considered. With Si, $\theta_n = 6$, and with Ge, $\theta_n = 4$.

lattice is solved for the energy eigenvalues in momentum space. The number of states in a given volume of momentum space equal g_s. However, as we are dealing with semiconductors, the density of electrons is normally so low that we may expand the energy about the minima and otherwise neglect the details of the eigenvalue solution. The eigenvalue calculation is feasible only for a perfect lattice in equilibrium, for reasons related to the discussion presented later with Fig. 11.2b, but that solution is sufficient to obtain the number θ_n.

The entropy of the system is described according to the Fermi–Dirac statistical model. In the s group, there are the following states:

$$z_1, z_2, z_3, z_4, z_5, \cdots, z_{g_s}$$

with occupation as designated directly below corresponding states:

$$z_1 \quad z_2 \quad z_3 \quad z_4 \quad z_5 \cdots z_{g_s}$$

$$0 \quad 1 \quad 0 \quad 0 \quad 1 \cdots 1$$

Hence we have n_s occupied states, $z_2, z_5, \cdots, z_{g_s}$ and $g_s - n_s$ empty states, e.g., $z_1, z_3, z_4, \cdots$, etc. Therefore the probability for a given arrangement of the system may be written

$$W = \prod_s \frac{g_s!}{(g_s - n_s)! \, n_s!} \qquad (112.3)$$

Inserting (112.3) into (111.1), evaluating factorial quantities by Stirling's approximation, $n! = (n/e)^n$, and maximizing (111.1) subject to (111.2), (111.3), and (112.1) gives the following modified Fermi distribution function, obtained earlier by Brillouin (1934):

$$f_s = \frac{n_s}{g_s} = [1 + \exp(\alpha_l + \beta_l E_s - \gamma_l q v_{s1})]^{-1} \quad (112.4)$$

in which α_l, β_l, γ_l are the Lagrangian multipliers associated with the conditional relations (111.2), (111.3), and (112.1), respectively.

The function f_s is symmetric about the origin in momentum space in the equilibrium case ($\gamma_l = 0$), but not in the non-

equilibrium case ($\gamma_l \neq 0$). This means that surfaces with
constant f are ellipsoidal in momentum space with centroids
at the minima with $\gamma_l = 0$, but displaced from the origin
with $\gamma_l \neq 0$. We now determine the amount that each
ellipsoidal surface with constant f is displaced from its
equilibrium location in momentum space, under the application of a field E directed along the p_1 axis.

Take any pair of energy minima in momentum space
oppositely displaced from the origin. These minima represent
Galilean frames traveling with equal and opposite velocity
with respect to the sample, and in equilibrium the net
velocity of the electrons retained in both minima vanishes.
We take an expansion of the energy about each minimum in
the differential values of velocity and momentum which are
the same for all minima, and it is these differentials to which
the symbols of velocity and momentum refer throughout the
text.

For the moment, consider the velocity v_{s1} classically as
$(1/m)_{11}p_{s1}$, and assume that the reciprocal mass tensor is
diagonalized by making the axes x_j ($j = 1, 2, 3$) coincide
with the principal axes of the ellipsoidal surfaces of constant
energy in momentum space,† so that the energy E_s may be
written

$$E_s = \frac{1}{2}\left[\left(\frac{1}{m}\right)_{11}p_{s1}^2 + \left(\frac{1}{m}\right)_{22}p_{s2}^2 + \left(\frac{1}{m}\right)_{33}p_{s3}^2\right] - q\varphi_i \quad (112.5)$$

Then, the exponent of (112.4) may be written

$$\Lambda_s = \alpha_l + \frac{\beta_l}{2}\left[\left(\frac{1}{m}\right)_{11}p_{s1}^2 + \left(\frac{1}{m}\right)_{22}p_{s2}^2 + \left(\frac{1}{m}\right)_{33}p_{s3}^2\right]$$

$$- \beta_l q\varphi_i - \gamma_l q\left(\frac{1}{m}\right)_{11}p_{s1} \quad (112.5a)$$

---

† These are spheroids in Si and Ge. Designating the axis of revolution
as $j = 1$, making axes $j = 2, 3$ lie in the equatorial plane, we have
$m_{11} \approx m$ for the (100) direction in Si, $m_{11} \approx 1.6m$ for the (111) direction
in Ge, and $m_{22} = m_{33} \approx 0.2m$ Si, $0.1m$ Ge.

which, by completing the square becomes

$$\Lambda_s = \alpha_l + \frac{\beta_l}{2}\left[\left(\frac{1}{m}\right)_{11}\left(p_{s1} - \frac{\gamma_l q}{\beta_l}\right)^2 + \left(\frac{1}{m}\right)_{22} p_{s2}{}^2 + \left(\frac{1}{m}\right)_{33} p_{s3}{}^2\right]$$

$$- \beta_l q \varphi_i - \frac{\gamma_l{}^2 q^2}{2\beta_l}\left(\frac{1}{m}\right)_{11} \quad (112.6)$$

It appears that α_l should be a constant for the entire system—yet in general it becomes a function $\alpha_l(x_1, x_2, x_3)$. This apparent paradox is explained by an inherent difference between equilibrium and nonequilibrium systems. The sum,

$$n = \sum_s n_s = \sum_s g_s f_s \quad (111.2)$$

which employs the Lagrangian multiplier α_l, cannot mean the same thing in the two cases. It does not matter in (111.2) that n can be $n(x_1, x_2, x_3)$ in an equilibrium system, because the number of particles in the system is constant, and (111.2) gives its average. The equilibrium potential $\varphi_i(x_1, x_2, x_3)$ alone gives the local fluctuation in particle density. Once equilibrium is upset, we can no longer specify α_l everywhere the same. In the steady state (111.2) applies to each separate space, so that α_l must become $\alpha_l(x_1, x_2, x_3)$. Not so with β_l and γ_l which have to do with mean energy, and flow, and which are constant throughout the system.

Inserting (112.6) into (112.4) shows that the centroids of the surfaces with constant f are now located at $p_{s1} = \gamma_l q/\beta_l$, $p_{s2} = p_{s3} = 0$. We know that the shift in momentum along the x_1 axis is the impulse $-qE\tau_s$ with E the constant field and τ_s the collision time of electrons in the s group. As the centroid of all concentric surfaces of constant f has been displaced by the same amount $\gamma_l q/\beta_l$, which must also equal $-qE\tau_s$, then the collision time $\tau_s = -\gamma_l/(\beta_l E)$ is independent of energy (the same for all groups) for small perturbations on the system, and may be written

$$\tau = -\gamma_l/(\beta_l E) \quad (112.7)$$

The constants $\alpha_l = -\zeta/(\kappa T)$, and $\beta_l = 1/(\kappa T)$ are treated in the extensive literature on the equilibrium case, and the constant γ_l follows from the last relation and (112.7), viz.,

$$\gamma_l = -E\tau/(\kappa T) \qquad (112.8\text{a})$$

The nonequilibrium version of α_l, which as remarked earlier is a function of coordinates, becomes

$$\alpha_l(x_1, x_2, x_3) = -\zeta_n(x_1, x_2, x_3)/(\kappa T) \qquad (112.8\text{b})$$

with $\zeta_n(x_1, x_2, x_3)$ the electrochemical potential of electrons (or quasi-Fermi level of electrons).

The following development of nonequilibrium statistics, which is after Lorentz, treats a system under steady flow as a perturbation of the equilibrium system. Consider the function f_s given by (112.4), which gives the probability of occupancy of the s group of states numbering g_s (hence $n_s = f_s g_s$). The total time derivative of f_s, related to variations in space and time coordinates, accounts for all particles leaving group s, e.g.,

$$\frac{df_s}{dt} = \sum_{j=1}^{3}\left[v_j \frac{\partial f_s}{\partial x_j} + \dot{p}_j \frac{\partial f_s}{\partial p_j} \right] + \frac{\partial f_s}{\partial t} \qquad (112.9)$$

In seeking a way to incorporate collision processes into (112.9), we digress to discuss electron interactions.

We ignore electron-electron interactions as these relate to internal forces which are incapable of moving the electronic system or increasing its energy. We consider outside forces such as applied fields, and collisions with lattice distortion through thermal motion (electron-phonon interactions).

Note that the internal energy of the lattice at given temperatures is high, as compared with electrons, (a) with metals, because the specific heat per electron is low compared with that of a lattice atom, (b) with semiconductors, because the number of charge carriers is small compared with the number of atoms. Thus, the lattice atoms act as a heat reservoir in contact with the electronic system. Except in substantial departure from the equilibrium state, the lattice maintains the temperature of the electronic system near its own through electron phonon collisions.

Consider the application of an outside force (applied field) which transforms the o group into the s group of states, and the s group into another, etc. If this transformation takes place by a relaxation process, with characteristic time τ, which should be proportional to the electron-phonon collision time, then we may write

$$\frac{\partial f_s}{\partial t} = \frac{(f_s - f_0)}{\tau} \qquad (112.10)$$

With a constant field E applied along axis 1, the steady state form of (112.9) reduces to†

$$-qE\frac{\partial f_s}{\partial p_1} + v_1\frac{\partial f_s}{\partial x_1} + \frac{(f_s - f_0)}{\tau} = 0 \qquad (112.11)$$

If the system is not perturbed very much from equilibrium (the relative magnitude of applied field is small with respect to internal fields), then we may write for f_s

$$f_s = f_0 + \frac{\partial f_0}{\partial p_1}dp_1 + \frac{\partial f_0}{\partial x_1}dx_1 \qquad (112.12)$$

which, through (112.11) may be approximated by equating the derivatives of f_s to those of f_0, e.g.

$$f_s = f_0 + qE\tau\frac{\partial f_0}{\partial p_1} - v_1\tau\frac{\partial f_0}{\partial x_1} \qquad (112.13)$$

---

† Under either a constant or oscillating applied field, the rates at which electrons enter and leave group s are equal, making df_s/dt vanish. The following descriptive statement is equivalent to (112.11):

$$\underset{\text{fields}}{(\partial f_s/\partial t)} + \underset{\text{collisions}}{(f_s - f_0)/\tau} = 0.$$

1.1.3. Current Density

The current density may be written

$$J_x = -q \langle nv_1 \rangle = J_{x0} + J_{x1} + J_{x2} \qquad (113.1)$$

in which the three terms correspond, respectively, to the contributions from the three terms in (112.13). We rewrite (113.1) in terms of (112.13):

$$J = \int_g \left[\underbrace{-qv_1 f_0}_{J_0} \underbrace{- q^2 E \tau v_1 \frac{\partial f_0}{\partial p_1}}_{J_1} + \underbrace{q \tau v_1{}^2 \frac{\partial f_0}{\partial x_1}}_{J_2} \right] dg \qquad (113.2)$$

Contribution J_0 vanishes because the Fermi distribution function f_0 is even and the velocity v_1 an odd function in momentum space.

To evaluate contribution J_1, we equate v_1 to $\partial E(\mathbf{p})/\partial p_1$ and integrate over one factor, dp_1 in dg:

$$\tau \int_{-\infty}^{\infty} \frac{\partial E}{\partial p_1} \frac{\partial f_0}{\partial p_1} dp_1 = \underbrace{\tau \frac{\partial E(\mathbf{p})}{\partial p_1} f_0 \Big|_{-\infty}^{\infty}}_{\text{vanishes}} - \tau \int_{-\infty}^{\infty} f_0 \frac{\partial^2 E(\mathbf{p})}{\partial p_1{}^2} dp_1 \quad (113.3)$$

Hence, by (113.3) and (113.2) we have the drift current density,

$$J_1 = q^2 E \tau \int_g f_0 \frac{\partial^2 E}{\partial p_1{}^2} dg = q^2 n \tau E / m^* \qquad (113.4)$$

in agreement with (103.2). Inserting the mobility μ_n (103.13) into (103.3) gives $q^2 n \tau / m^*$ for the conductivity, and therefore (113.4) is a statement of Ohm's law $J_1 = \sigma_n E$.

The term J_2 may be written immediately:

$$J_2 = q \tau \langle v_1{}^2 \rangle \frac{\partial n}{\partial x} \qquad (113.5)$$

With small fields, justifying the type of calculation used here, the mean square velocity of electrons is about the same as without the field. Hence $\langle v_1{}^2 \rangle$ only slightly exceeds $v^2/3$, with

$$v^2 = \langle v_1{}^2 + v_2{}^2 + v_3{}^2 \rangle = 3\langle v_1{}^2 \rangle \qquad (113.6)$$

expressing the equilibrium case. We equate the product $v\tau$ to λ, the mean free path of electrons, and write the diffusion current density,

$$J_2 = q\left(\frac{v\lambda}{3}\right)\frac{\partial n}{\partial x} = qD_n\frac{\partial n}{\partial x} \qquad (113.7)$$

in agreement with (103.4) and verifying the expression for the diffusion coefficient stated earlier, (103.5). Taking $-q\varphi_n$ as the electrochemical potential for electrons, then n may be written $n_i \exp q(\varphi_i - \varphi_n)/\kappa T$, which together with (113.7) and the Einstein relation (103.12) yields

$$J_2 = \sigma_n\frac{\partial(\varphi_i - \varphi_n)}{\partial x_1} \qquad (113.8)$$

while (113.4) becomes

$$J_1 = -\sigma_n\frac{\partial\varphi_i}{\partial x_1} \qquad (113.9)$$

so that we have, for the total current density,

$$J = J_1 + J_2 = -\sigma_n\frac{\partial\varphi_n}{\partial x} \qquad (113.10)$$

Hence, if the material is homogeneous (n constant), then (113.8) must vanish and (113.9) and (113.10) must be equivalent, requiring $\varphi_i(x)$ and $\varphi_n(x)$ to be the same linear function of x apart from a constant.

Take a homogeneous system in a steady state in which the nonequilibrium Fermi distribution function is represented by f_0 with a small oscillation $f_1 \exp i\omega t$ superimposed, as a result of a sinusoidal applied field $E \exp i\omega t$. In this case $\partial f_s/\partial t$ in (112.9) contains in addition to (112.10) the following oscillating component:

$$\left(\frac{\partial f_s}{\partial t}\right)' = i\omega f_1 \exp i\omega t = i\omega(f_s - f_0) \qquad (113.11)$$

Instead of (112.11), we have for the ac case

$$-qEe^{i\omega t}\frac{\partial f_s}{\partial p_1} + i\omega(f_s - f_0) + (f_s - f_0)/\tau = 0 \quad (113.12)$$

which becomes in the first order approximation

$$f_s = f_0 + \frac{q\tau Ee^{i\omega t}}{1 + i\omega\tau}\frac{\partial f_0}{\partial p_1} \quad (113.13)$$

Accordingly, we have $\sigma_{dc}(1 + i\omega\tau)^{-1}$ for the ac conductivity.

It is pertinent to discuss arguments for testing the validity of the perturbation method of treating the steady flow of electrons. For the sake of simplicity, in the remainder of the text it is assumed that crystal symmetry permits the ellipsoidal surfaces of constant energy in momentum space to reduce to spherical surfaces, i.e., $(1/m)_{11} = (1/m)_{22} = (1/m)_{33}$. According to simple particle mechanics, a unit volume of the system moves past a stationary observer with the velocity of flow $\langle v \rangle = -\mu E$, which is the velocity of the centroid of the population. Let the velocity of the ith electron with respect to the centroid be $\mathbf{v}_i$. The energy density of the population is given by the expression

$$u = \sum_i \frac{m}{2}|\mathbf{v}_i|^2 + \frac{nm}{2}\langle v \rangle^2 \quad (113.14)$$

The increase in energy due to the field is given by the second term, which amounts to $(m/2)(\mu E)^2$ per electron. For the perturbation calculations, (112.9)–(113.13), to have validity, the second term must be small compared with the first. As an example, take a nondegenerate n-type semiconductor. In this case, a classical interpretation of (113.14) is appropriate, and the ratio of the 2nd to the 1st term may be written $(qE\lambda/3\kappa T)^2$. This ratio is small at room temperature for weak fields, e.g., $\lambda = 10^3$ Å and $E \ll 7500$ volts/cm. It is interesting to note that the energy $q\lambda E$ is removed from the field and transferred to the lattice by the electron in one mean free path, but the total increase in energy of the electron is $m(\mu E)^2/2 = (q\lambda E)^2/2mv^2$. Hence, the energy increase per electron from the field is $(q\lambda E/2mv^2)$, or (energy gain by the lattice from one mean free path of the electron)/ (four times the total energy of the electron), times the energy received by the lattice in one mean free path, which is a small fraction for weak fields.

Another relation, which illustrates that the increase in energy of the electrons from the field E is small, is obtained by writing the second term of (113.14) as $\sigma E^2 \tau / 2$. Noting that the density of power dissipation is σE^2 and that $\tau \sim 10^{-13}$ sec, it is clear that the increase in energy density of electrons is very small. Thus, practically all energy delivered from the external field E, at the rate σE^2 is transferred from the electrons to the lattice, almost none being retained by the electrons.

Although the increase in energy per electron by the field E is small compared with $1/40$ of an electron volt at room temperature, the potential variation across the system from the applied field may be several volts. The question to be answered is the following. How does an applied potential difference appear in the function f_s as stated in (112.4)?

1.1.4. Potential Distribution

Consider a semiconducting sample in which the charge density vanishes, and the impurity concentration is uniform, as determined over regions enclosing around 10^{12} atoms. If a potential difference is applied across the sample, the potential within is the solution of Poisson's equation with vanishing charge density, i.e., a linear function of the distance. However, on the scale of lattice spacing, the charge density does not vanish and the potential varies periodically with the lattice spacing, and this periodic potential is superimposed on the linear potential applied externally. Again, there may be random fluctuations in charge density, resulting from local fluctuations in impurity concentration, with a mean separation of several hundred lattice spacings. Once more, there is a fluctuating potential superimposed on a linear potential applied externally. Let $\varphi_{s1}(x)$ represent the perturbing potential, over the range of the variable, $0 < x < L_0$, produced by the applied field E, which is constant as averaged over distances of the order of 10^4 lattice spacings. Let the unperturbed potential in the sample be $\varphi_{i0}(x)$, which may fluctuate as was just discussed. To the potential $\varphi_{i0}(x)$ is added the small perturbation $\varphi_{i1}(x)$ from the constant applied field $E = -d\varphi_{i1}/dx = -\varphi_{i1}(L_0)/L_0$. Hence, $\varphi_{i1}(x) = \varphi_{i1}(L_0)x/L_0$ is the perturbing potential, and the total potential may be written

$$\varphi_i(x) = \varphi_{i0}(x) + \varphi_{i1}(L_0)x/L_0 \qquad (114.1)$$

Let ζ represent the Fermi level of the sample with no applied field, and let

$$\zeta_n(x) = \zeta + \zeta_1(x) \qquad (114.2)$$

represent the quasi-Fermi level, or electrochemical potential, of the electrons with an applied field. The exponent $(\alpha_l + \beta_l E_s - \gamma_l q v_{s1})$ within the modified Fermi distribution function (112.4) may be written in terms of (114.1) and (114.2) as follows:

$$\Lambda(x) = -\frac{\zeta + \zeta_1(x)}{\kappa T} + \frac{|\mathbf{p}|^2}{2m\kappa T} + \frac{qE\tau v_1}{\kappa T}$$

$$-\frac{q}{\kappa T}\left[\varphi_{i0}(x) + \frac{\varphi_{i1}(L_0)x}{L_0}\right] \qquad (114.3)$$

The population of electrons will be the same as without the field, and hence the modified Fermi distribution function must remain constant. Therefore, the sum of terms in (114.3) added by the applied field must vanish, e.g.,

$$-\frac{\zeta_1(x)}{\kappa T} - \frac{q\varphi_{i1}(L_0)x}{\kappa T L_0} + \frac{qv_1\tau E}{\kappa T} = 0 \qquad (114.4)$$

As the last term is normally negligible compared with the other two on the basis of arguments given in Section 1.1.3 the quasi-Fermi level may be written

$$\zeta_n(x) = \zeta - \frac{q\varphi_{i1}(L_0)x}{L_0} \qquad (114.5)$$

in agreement with the conclusion drawn after Eq. (113.10).

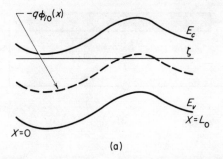

(a)

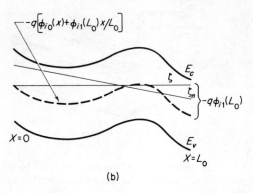

(b)

FIG. 11.1. (a) Electron energy band diagram for an inhomogenous semiconductor in equilibrium. (b) Electron energy band diagram for the same region, shown in (a) except under the application of a uniform electric field.

Figures 11.1a and 11.1b illustrate the effect of an applied field on the energy bands and quasi-Fermi level. Hence, the equilibrium relations (102.1) and (102.5) may be modified to treat the nonequilibrium case by replacing ζ, in (102.1), by ζ_n, and, in (102.5), by ζ_p, e.g.,

$$n = n_i \exp(\zeta_n - \zeta_i)/\kappa T \qquad (114.6)$$

and

$$p = n_i \exp(\zeta_i - \zeta_p)/\kappa T \qquad (114.7)$$

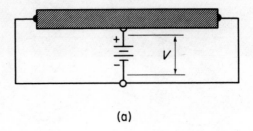

(a)

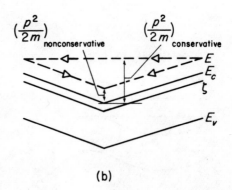

(b)

Fig. 11.2. (a) A semiconducting sample connected to a battery. (b) Electron energy band diagram for the semiconducting sample shown. in (a).

Consider a uniform semiconducting sample, connected across a battery as shown in Fig. 11.2a. The energy band diagram corresponding to this case appears in Fig. 11.2b in which the energy of a particular electron is indicated for a conservative system (straight line) and a nonconservative system (V-shaped line). The purpose of including Fig. 11.2 is to illustrate that although we use a free electron model of conduction electrons in the semiconductor, the electrons do not respond to an applied potential difference as if they were free. For example, in the non-conservative system, the kinetic energy $(p^2/2m)$ remains about the same throughout the semiconductor, whereas in the conservative system it increases with the applied potential difference. Actually, this situation is not out of harmony with the free electron model, but a natural consequence of it. The free electron model applies to electronic behavior in a perfect crystal, and hence in an actual crystal it applies only to the behavior between collisions. It is implied in the discussion connected with (113.14) that over large distances with respect to a mean free path, the energy E follows the V-shaped line in Fig. 11.2b.

1.2. Nonequilibrium Carrier Concentrations

1.2.1. Local Region Optically Excited

Consider a transient excess in hole and electron concentration in a small region, as a result of that region being exposed to a flash of light. The discussion concerns an n-type sample, and it is assumed that the sample meets the following conditions:

(1) The charge density vanishes, as averaged over regions containing $\sim 10^9$ atoms,

(2) The potential is constant as averaged over linear distances of $\sim 10^3$ Å.

(3) The temperature is constant.

(4) Electrons and holes have equal mobility ($\mu_n = \mu_p$).

The local increase in carrier concentration is illustrated in the energy band diagram, Fig. 12.1.

The region, in which the Fermi level branches into the electrochemical potentials ζ_n and ζ_p for electrons and holes, is where the excess charge carrier concentration is localized. Within the dielectric relaxation time ϵ/σ, which is normally small with respect to the electron-hole recombination time, the excess concentration of electrons is matched in every part of the region by an equal excess concentration of holes, $\Delta n = \Delta_p$, making the net charge practically vanish.

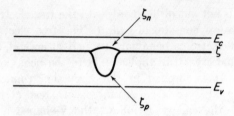

FIG. 12.1. Electron energy band diagram, showing a region in which large excess carrier concentrations have been optically induced. The electrochemical potentials of the electrons and holes depart in this region in order to account for the excess carrier concentrations.

We are at liberty to let $\zeta_i = 0$ in (114.6) and (114.7) so that the nonequilibrium concentrations of electrons and holes may be accounted for by only their electrochemical potentials ζ_n and ζ_p according to the following statements:

$$n = n_i \exp \zeta_n/\kappa T \qquad (121.1)$$

and

$$p = n_i \exp -\zeta_p/\kappa T \qquad (121.2)$$

These relations are illustrated schematically in Fig. 12.2. As the excess carrier concentrations $\Delta n = n - n_0$, and $\Delta p = p - p_0$ are maintained almost equal through Coulomb forces, one may take the differentials of (121.1) and (121.2),

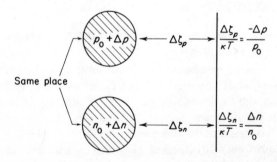

FIG. 12.2. Illustration of a region containing excess carrier concentrations, showing the variations in the electrochemical potentials.

and equate them on the basis of charge neutrality; the result is the following relation:

$$\Delta \zeta_p = -(n_0 \Delta \zeta_n)/p_0 \qquad (121.3)$$

which governs the variations in the electrochemical potentials ζ_n and ζ_p in such a way that they depart from the equilibrium value of ζ in opposite directions, and, of the two, the electrochemical potential of the minority carriers departs further (Fig. 12.1). The restriction $\mu_n = \mu_p$ is removed in the next section, in which it is explained that a shift in band edges must occur where equilibrium is upset.

1.2.2. Dember Effect

In general the mobility of electrons differs from that of holes, which gives rise to the *Dember potential* (Dember, 1931) a small potential difference between a region with a nonequilibrium carrier concentration and one with the equilibrium concentration. The Dember potential arises through the Coulomb attraction which restrains the more mobile excess carriers from diffusing away from the less mobile carriers.

The Dember potential is measured across ohmic contacts at the sample boundaries $x = 0, L_0$, with an indicator of very high resistance compared with the sample. It is assumed in the following derivation that the sample is uniform, and with such a sample the Dember potential appears when the sample is illuminated nonuniformly. To partially cancel nonuniformities in the sample and end contacts, one may take the average of the two Dember potentials measured with the light spot first at one end ($x = 0$) and then transferred to the other ($x = L_0$). The band diagram of the sample under illumination is shown in Fig. 12.3 for the case $\mu_n > \mu_p$. The variation with distance x of the separation between the electrochemical potential for electrons ζ_n and the edge of the conduction band E_c indicates that the concentration of electrons is greatest at the center of the light spot ($x = L_0$),

58 1. Properties of Electrons in Crystals

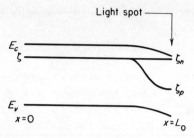

FIG. 12.3. Electron energy band diagram for a semiconducting sample which is in equilibrium except in the region of the boundary on the right, $x = L_0$, where there is an excess concentration of carriers.

and decreases with decreasing x to the equilibrium concentration at the point where the electrochemical potentials ζ_n and ζ_p merge into the equilibrium Fermi level ζ. As the holes are minority carriers, it follows from (121.3) that ζ_p departs more from the equilibrium value ζ than ζ_n (Fig. 12.3).

Let the equilibrium concentrations of electrons and holes be denoted as n_0 and p_0 and the excess hole concentration $p(x) - p_0 = p_1(x)$. We assume charge neutrality making $n(x) - n_0 = p_1(x)$. Adding the current density of electrons,

$$J_n = -q\mu_n n\frac{d\varphi_i}{dx} + qD_n\frac{dn}{dx} \qquad (122.1)$$

to that of holes,

$$J_p = -q\mu_p p\frac{d\varphi_i}{dx} - qD_p\frac{dp}{dx} \qquad (122.2)$$

yields the total current density which must vanish, as the samples look into an open circuit. As a result, we have the differential equation

$$(\mu_p - \mu_n)\frac{\kappa T}{q}\frac{dp_1}{d\varphi_i} + [(\mu_p p_0 + \mu_n n_0) + (\mu_p + \mu_n)p_1] = 0$$

$$(122.3)$$

Taking $p_1(0) = 0$ for the boundary condition, and letting $\varphi_i(0) = 0$, we have for the solution of (122.3)

$$\varphi_i(x) = \left(\frac{\mu_n - \mu_p}{\mu_n + \mu_p}\right)\frac{\kappa T}{q} \ln\left(\frac{\sigma(x)}{\sigma_0}\right) \qquad (122.4)$$

with $\sigma(x) = [\mu_n n(x) + \mu_p p(x)]q$, and $\sigma_0 = (\mu_n n_0 + \mu_p p_0)q$ denoting the instantaneous and equilibrium conductivities, respectively. The potential $\varphi_i(L_0)$ was measured with samples of n-type and p-type germanium by Stubbe and Gossick (1958), and the ratio $\mu_n/\mu_p = 2.1$, obtained by evaluating the results according to (122.4), was in good agreement with the same ratio based on measurements of drift mobility reported by Prince (1953).

1.2.3. Photovoltaic Effect

As before, consider an excess of hole and electron concentration generated by a light spot, except that the region under consideration is a $p - n$ junction (Becker and Fan, 1950). The terminals of the junction are not connected, so that the total current density vanishes. The situation is illustrated in the energy band diagram in Fig. 12.4. The following relations may be written on the basis of (114.6) and (114.7):

$$n_p p_p = n_{p0} p_{p0} \exp(\zeta_n - \zeta_p)/\kappa T, \qquad x = x_p \quad (123.1)$$

and

$$n_n p_n = n_{n0} p_{n0} \exp(\zeta_n - \zeta_p)/\kappa T, \qquad x = x_n \quad (123.2)$$

If it is assumed that the excess carrier densities are not great, i.e., that on the p side $n_p \ll p_{p0}$ making $p_p \sim p_{p0}$, and on the n side $p_n \ll n_{n0}$, making $n_n \sim n_{n0}$, then (123.1) and (123.2) together yield the relations

$$(\zeta_n - \zeta_p) \approx \kappa T \ln p_n/p_{n0}, \qquad x = x_n \quad (123.3)$$

and

$$(\zeta_n - \zeta_p) \approx \kappa T \ln n_p/n_{p0}, \qquad x = x_p \quad (123.4)$$

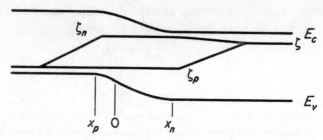

FIG. 12.4. Electron energy band diagram for a p-n junction, with an excess concentration of charge carriers in the region of the junction.

In this instance both the hole concentration on the n side and electron concentration on the p side have been multiplied by a factor $\exp(\zeta_n - \zeta_p)/\kappa T$. Consequently the separation between $E_c(x_p)$ and $E_c(x_n)$ has been reduced by an amount $\sim(\zeta_n - \zeta_p)$, making an external potential difference appear across the terminals of the junction, a photo emf V, with qV equal to $(\zeta_n - \zeta_p)$ as given by (123.3) or (123.4).

Let us consider a greater excess minority carrier concentration by a treatment that holds for those applications which fall in either of the following two categories:

(1) a p-n junction which has much more impure material on one side than on the other, or

(2) a metal-semiconductor rectifying barrier.

Take, for example, a p-n junction with the p side very impure compared with the n side, or a metal-n-type semiconductor barrier. For the former, Fig. 12.4 gives an appropriate energy band diagram, and for the latter, see Fig. 20.3a. We remove the restriction $p_n \ll n_{n0}$ in the n-type material outside the barrier, but retain the assumption of charge neutrality in that region.

It may be seen, by inspecting Fig. 12.4 or Fig. 20.3a, that the potential difference across the exterior terminals of either rectifying system (the photo emf) is given by the shift in the electrochemical potential for holes at the n

boundary according to the relation

$$V = (\zeta - \zeta_p)/q \qquad (123.5)$$

with the right side of (123.5) evaluated for $x = x_n$ in Fig. 12.4, or $x = w$ in Fig. 20.3a. It follows from (114.7) and (123.5) that the hole concentration on the n boundary is related to the photo emf V by the following expression:

$$V = \frac{\kappa T}{q} \ln \frac{p_n}{p_{n0}} \qquad (123.6)$$

Furthermore, the neutrality condition $n_n - n_{n0} = p_n - p_{n0}$, the relations $n_{n0}p_{n0} = n_i^2$, and (123.6) together yield the following expression which relates the electron concentration at the n boundary to the photo emf:

$$V = \frac{\kappa T}{q} \ln[1 + (n_n - n_{n0})n_{n0}n_i^{-2}] \qquad (123.7)$$

As a small effect, the Dember potential adds to or subtracts from the photovoltaic shift in the barrier, depending on whether the mobility of electrons is greater or less than that of holes.

1.2.4. Recombination Process

A local excess concentration of carriers vanishes by two processes: leakage out of the region by diffusion, and decay by hole-electron recombination. The diffusion process has already been discussed, and attention here is confined to the second process, viz., recombination.

Both the generation and recombination of electron-hole pairs occur simultaneously in semiconductors, and in equilibrium the two rates are equal. Consider the recombination rate of holes, which may be written, in terms of kinetic theory as

$$\Upsilon = N_r \Sigma p v_{\text{diff}} \qquad (124.1)$$

with N_r and Σ the density and cross section of recombination centers, and v_{diff} the diffusion velocity of holes. The spectral width of recombination radiation is too narrow to permit a recombination transition to occur while a hole makes one pass by a recombination center with thermal velocity. It must remain in the region of a recombination center, as in the diffusion process, for a time for recombination to occur. The generation rate

$$G = N_r \Sigma p_0 v_{\text{diff}} \qquad (124.2)$$

with p_0 the equilibrium concentration of holes, because $G = \Upsilon$ at equilibrium.

We let τ_p stand for $(N_r \Sigma v_{\text{diff}})^{-1}$, and call it the *recombination time of holes*:

$$\tau_p = 1/(N_r \Sigma v_{\text{diff}}) \qquad (124.3)$$

The collision time has been denoted τ in earlier sections. As the collision time and recombination time are not similar and rarely considered in the same discussion, it should be clear from the context which time is denoted by τ_p.

Inserting (124.3) into (124.1) and (124.2) and taking the difference, gives the decay rate of the nonequilibrium hole concentration, viz.,

$$dp/dt = G - \Upsilon = -(p - p_0)/\tau_p \qquad (124.4)$$

The differential equation (124.4) has the well-known solution

$$p(t) - p_0 = [p(0) - p_0] \exp -t/\tau_p \qquad (124.5)$$

showing the excess concentration to decay according to the relaxation law.

The recombination time with very pure material may be as high as 1000 μsec with germanium and 100 μsec with silicon.

1.2.5. Reduction in Excess Carrier Concentration through Both Diffusion and Recombination

A steady state nonequilibrium hole concentration is considered in this section (the case with $dp/dt = 0$). Take a one-dimensional case with $x = w$ the boundary of a *p-n*

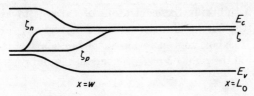

FIG. 12.5. Electron energy band diagram for a *p-n* junction, with an excess concentration of charge carriers in the region of the junction.

junction and $x = L_0$ the other boundary of the sample. The region, $w < x < L_0$, is a uniform *n*-type semiconductor. The energy band diagram (Fig. 12.5) refers to the sample under discussion. The following conditions also apply:

(I) A potential difference V is applied across the sample, reducing the height of the potential barrier from its equilibrium value V_B to $(V_B - V)$. Thus, on the basis of the discussion in Section 1.2.3, and the construction of Fig. 12.5, the applied voltage V is related to the electrochemical potentials ζ_n and ζ_p by the expression

$$qV = (\zeta_n - \zeta_p)_{x=w} \qquad (125.0)$$

(II) Taking the current flow through the sample as I, and the resistance over the length $w < x < L_0$ as R, the relation $IR \ll V$ is satisfied, so that essentially all the potential is taken up in charging the barrier capacitance sufficiently to reduce the barrier from its equilibrium height V_B to $V_B - V$. (Charging the barrier capacitance consists in reducing the barrier width by adding a layer of electrons on the right to neutralize ionized donors, and a layer of holes on the left to neutralize ionized acceptors, the number of electrons in the added layer on the right being equal to the number of holes in the layer added on the left. The displacement of the barrier from its equilibrium height permits a nonequilibrium concentration of carriers to appear in the barrier and the surrounding region.)

(III) The hole concentration at the boundary of the region on the right ($x = L_0$) equals the equilibrium value p_0

$$p(L_0) = p_0 \qquad (125.1)$$

(IV) The equilibrium hole concentration p_0 and excess hole concentration $p_1 = p - p_0$ are both small compared with the equilibrium concentration of electrons n_0. Hence we may write the boundary condition

$$p(w) = p_0 \exp[(\zeta_n - \zeta_p)/\kappa T] = p_0 \exp(qV/\kappa T) \qquad (125.2)$$

(V) The sample length is very long compared with the diffusion length of holes, or

$$\sqrt{D_p \tau_p} \ll L_0 \qquad (125.3)$$

Note that if condition (V) is removed, then (III) is subject to the simplifying assumption that the nature of the contact at $x = L_0$ maintains the hole concentration constant at the equilibrium value p_0.

We consider the steady state flow of holes, injected into the n side from the barrier at $x = w$. By condition (II) the potential φ_i is constant throughout ($w < x < L_0$), and therefore the drift term of the hole current vanishes. Hence, we may write the density of hole current as

$$J_p = -qD_p \frac{\partial p_1}{\partial x} \qquad (125.4)$$

With the steady flow of holes, the continuity equation of excess hole concentration takes the form

$$-\frac{\partial p_1}{\partial t} = 0 = \frac{1}{q}\frac{\partial J_p}{\partial x} + \frac{p_1}{\tau_p}, \qquad w < x < L_0 \qquad (125.5)$$

Inserting (125.4) into (125.5), yields the following ordinary differential equation:

$$\frac{d^2 p_1}{dx^2} - \frac{p_1}{D_p \tau_p} = 0, \qquad w < x < L_0 \qquad (125.6)$$

which has the solution

$$p(x) = A \exp(-x/\sqrt{D_p \tau_p}) + B \exp(x/\sqrt{D_p \tau_p}) \qquad (125.7)$$

Boundary conditions (III) and (IV) make constants A and B satisfy the statements

$$A = p_1(w), \qquad \text{and} \qquad B = 0 \qquad (125.8)$$

Therefore (125.7) may be written

$$p_1(x) = [p(w) - p_0] \exp[(w - x)/\sqrt{D_p \tau_p}],$$
$$w < x < L_0 \qquad (125.9)$$

In order to estimate the dependence of the electrochemical potential $\varphi_n(x)$ on x, we introduce condition (IV), stated by (125.2), through which we may write (125.9) as follows:

$$p_1(x) = p_0[\exp(qV/\kappa T) - 1] \exp[(w - x)/\sqrt{D_p \tau_p}]$$
$$(125.10)$$

At the same time $p(x)$ may be related to the equilibrium concentration p_0 through the electrochemical potentials, or quasi-Fermi levels, $\varphi_p(x)$ and $\varphi_n(x)$, by the statement

$$p(x) = p_0 \exp q[\varphi_p(x) - \varphi_n]/\kappa T \qquad (125.11)$$

It should be stated that (125.11) is an approximation in which a slight dependence of φ_n on x is ignored through condition (II), and it has been assumed, through condition (IV), that, over the range $w < x$, the difference $\varphi_n - \varphi_p$ is entirely taken up by the variation in φ_p from the equilibrium value φ. Further, in (125.2) we have assumed φ_p to be constant throughout the barrier. However, φ_p cannot be constant in the barrier, as this would require hole current to vanish.

Thus, φ_p must have a small slope throughout the barrier, to preserve the continuity of current density for reasons based on (113.10). With commercial germanium or silicon p-n junctions, (125.2) and (125.4) are good approximations.

The following expression for the electrochemical potential of holes is based on (125.10) and (125.11):

$$\varphi_p(x) - \varphi_n = V - \kappa T(x - w)/(q\sqrt{D_p\tau_p}), \qquad w < x$$

$$(125.12)$$

with $|\varphi_p(x) - \varphi_n| \gg \kappa T/q$, and this relation justifies the linear characteristic of $\zeta_p(x)$ shown in Fig. 12.5. The corresponding expression, for low excess hole concentration, also follows from (125.10) and (125.11):

$$\varphi_p(x) - \varphi_n = \frac{\kappa T}{q}[\exp(qV/\kappa T) - 1]\exp[(w-x)/\sqrt{D_p\tau_p}]$$

$$(125.13)$$

with $|\varphi_p(x) - \varphi_n| \ll \kappa T/q$. Both (125.12) and (125.13) indicate that the steeper the slope of the electrochemical potential, $\varphi_p(x) = -\zeta_p(x)/q$, the more brief the recombination time τ_p [e.g., see $\zeta_p(x)$ in Fig. 12.5].

The density of hole current may be written, on the basis of (125.4) and (125.10)

$$J_p(x) = qp_1(x)\sqrt{D_p/\tau_p} \qquad (125.14)$$

and as the current density may be written in general as the product of $qp_1(x)$ and velocity, it follows that the excess hole concentration moves to the right with a diffusion velocity

$$v_{\text{diff}} = \sqrt{D_p/\tau_p} \qquad (125.15)$$

Therefore, substituting $v\lambda/3$ for D_p, from (113.7) in (125.15) and letting λ/τ, with τ the collision time of holes, stand for v, we have for the ratio of diffusion velocity to thermal velocity v,

$$v_{\text{diff}}/v = \sqrt{\tau/3\tau_p} = \lambda/(3\sqrt{D_p\tau_p}) \qquad (125.16)$$

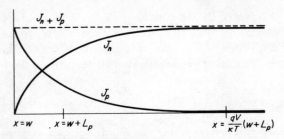

FIG. 12.6. Current density of electrons J_n, and current density of holes J_n, plotted against distance from the barrier.

which is very small in typical cases with germanium and silicon at room temperature (of the order of 10^{-5}). The quantity

$$L_p = \sqrt{D_p \tau_p} = 1/(N_r \Sigma) \qquad (125.17)$$

in (125.16) is called the *diffusion length* of holes. Equation (125.14) may also be written

$$J_p(x) = q p_1(w) \left(\frac{D_p}{\tau_p}\right)^{\frac{1}{2}} \exp\left(\frac{w - x}{L_p}\right) \qquad (125.18)$$

To maintain constant current density, through Kirchhoff's law, $J_n(x)$ must increase with x to compensate for the decrease in $J_p(x)$, as illustrated in Fig. 12.6. With an applied voltage $V \gg \kappa T/q$, it follows from (125.12) that the majority of excess holes decay in the range $w < x < w + qVL_p/\kappa T$. The electrons which recombine, through the recombination centers, with these holes are supplied by the electrons in $J_n(x)$ flowing to the left.

1.2.6. Thin Base Sample

Consider the steady flow of excess holes from a planar *p-n* junction, with the boundary on the *n* side at $x = w$, into the neutral *n*-type region with the extreme boundary at $x = L_0 \ll \sqrt{D_p \tau_p}$, i.e., into a *thin base*. This is like the problem considered in the previous section except that condition

(V) is replaced by the condition $L_0 \ll \sqrt{D_p \tau_p}$. In this case, the probability that an increment of excess hole concentration Δp_1 leaves the sample through recombination is small, because, according to (125.9), it must conform to the relation

$$\left| \frac{\Delta p_1}{p_1} \right| = \frac{L_0}{\sqrt{D_p \tau_p}} \ll 1 \qquad (126.1)$$

There is a tendency for the ohmic contact at $x = L_0$ to maintain a local equilibrium between the metal and the semiconductor at the contact to satisfy boundary condition (III) of the previous section.

It follows from (126.1) that the term p_1/τ_p vanishes in (125.5) making (125.6) reduce to

$$d^2 p_1/dx^2 = 0 \qquad (126.2)$$

which has the linear solution

$$p_1(x) = [p(w) - p_0](L_0 - x)/(L_0 - w),$$

$$w < x < L_0 \qquad (126.3)$$

The current density of holes, which follows from (125.4) and (126.3),

$$J_p(x) = \frac{qD_p}{(L_0 - w)}[p(w) - p_0] \qquad (126.4)$$

is independent of x. Thus, electron current is not required to make total current density constant—but, after all, recombination was neglected.

1.2.7. Photocurrent

Suppose that in either Section 1.2.5 or 1.2.6 the source of emf were replaced by a short circuit, and the barrier illuminated by a spot of light at $x = w$ of sufficient intensity to made the excess hole concentration the same as before. As the conditions of the problem are unchanged in the p-n junctions, the same solutions hold. The shift in barrier height

V, as it relates to excess hole concentration, is the same as before, except that it is controlled by light intensity instead of a source of emf.

A detailed review of photo effects in semiconductors has been presented by Tauc (1962).

Exercises

(1.1) Consider an n-type semiconductor, in which there is a steady state nonequilibrium distribution of electrons and holes. The excess hole concentration Δp is everywhere small compared with the equilibrium electron concentration n_0. Starting with the equations of continuity for excess hole and electron concentration, obtain the relation

$$\nabla \cdot \mathbf{J}_p = -\nabla \cdot \mathbf{J}_n = \frac{-qp_0}{\tau_p}\{\exp[q(\varphi_p - \varphi_n)/\kappa T] - 1\}$$

(1.2) Show that the short-circuit photo current may be determined by either of the circuits shown here.

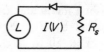 

The symbol ─◁─ represents the rectifying barrier, which carries a current $I(V)$ as a function of voltage applied across the barrier. R_s = series resistance of semiconductor pellet outside the barrier. L = emf generated by the absorbed light. $I_L = L/R_s$ = output of a current generator.

(1.3) Show that the short-circuit photo current is proportional to light intensity, assuming the latter to be uniformly absorbed over the area of the barrier.

CHAPTER 2

Boundary Double Layer

2.0. Potential Barrier at a Semiconductor Boundary

At the boundary of a semiconductor, either at a free surface, or between a semiconductor and a metal, or between a semiconductor of one type and that of the opposite type, there is in general a double layer as indicated in Figs. 20.1a and 20.1b. A typical double layer at the surface of an n-type semiconductor is illustrated in Fig. 20.1a. The negative surface charge consists of electrons trapped in boundary states, while the positive charge layer consists of ionized donor impurities which are uncompensated by conduction electrons. Everywhere else in the semiconductor the mean density of conduction electrons matches the density of donor impurities, so that the sample is electrically neutral. The double layer at the boundary between a metal and an n-type semiconductor may be also illustrated by Fig. 20.1a, and the physical description given for Fig. 20.1a also applies except that in addition to the charged boundary states of the semiconductor, electrons can collect at the surface of the metal as an electric image of the ionized donor impurities. Fig. 20.1b illustrates the double layer at the boundary of a p-n junction of the type produced by changing the impurity concentration while the crystal is being grown. In this instance, the double layer is composed of uncompensated ionized donor impurities on the right, and uncompensated ionized acceptor impurities on the left.

A potential barrier naturally accompanies the double layer at the boundary of a semiconductor. Depending upon the characteristic properties and history of the materials, the potential barrier at a boundary may have a wide variety of heights and widths. Figure 20.2 shows the potential barrier of a double layer in equilibrium. If the height is of the order

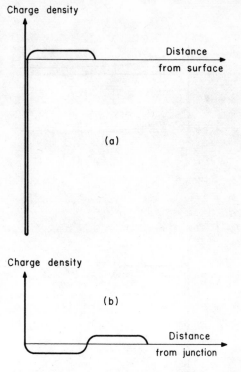

Fig. 20.1. (a) Charge density plotted against distance for a double layer at the free surface of a semiconductor. This diagram also applies to the double layer at a metal-semiconductor interface. (b) Charge density plotted against distance for the double layer associated with a p-n junction.

of or less than the thermal energy in electron volts $(V_B \gtrsim \kappa T/q)$, it is easily surmounted by conduction electrons or holes and does not function effectively as a barrier. Therefore, the discussion here is limited to those barriers which have a height much greater than $\kappa T/q$. Furthermore, if the width w of a barrier is of the order of or less than the wavelength of a conduction electron or hole, these charge carriers may tunnel through, and the barrier does not serve effectively as a barrier. For this reason, the discussion will be

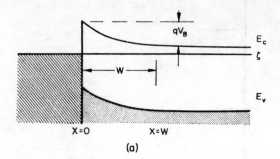

(a)

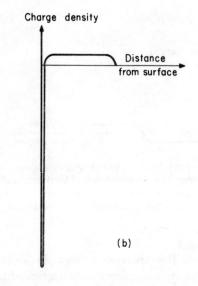

(b)

Fig. 20.2. (a) Electron energy band diagram for a metal-semiconductor barrier in equilibrium. [From Gossick (1963).] (b) Charge
density plotted against distance for a metal-semiconductor barrier in
equilibrium.

limited to those barriers which are much wider than the wavelength of charge carriers, i.e., of the order of several thousand angstroms.

When the equilibrium of a potential barrier is upset by the application of an external source of emf, making the potential difference between the two sides of the junction depart from the equilibrium value, the double layer contracts if the potential difference has been decreased, and expands if the potential difference has been increased. Figure 20.3a shows the conduction and valence electron energy band edges and Fig. 20.3b the charge density of a double layer with positive applied voltage V, which decreases the potential difference across the junction to $(V_B - V)$. The electrochemical potential for electrons $\zeta_n(x)$ has a dependence on distance similar to the electrochemical potential for holes $\zeta_p(x)$, in Fig. 20.3a, but this similarity depends on the manner in which the excess electrons injected into the metal are specified. Actually, the electrochemical potential for the density of all conduction electrons in the metal remains everywhere practically at the equilibrium Fermi level. However, by considering the excess population of electrons injected into the metal from the semiconductor separately, then the electrochemical potential for these electrons can assume a variety of values, and it is the electrochemical potential defined in this special sense that is shown in Fig. 20.3a. Figure 20.4a shows the conduction and valence energy band edges and Fig. 20.4b the charge density of a double layer which has had the potential difference across the junction increased by negative applied voltage. Positive applied voltage, which reduces the barrier height, is referred to as *forward bias*, while negative applied voltage, which increases the barrier height, is referred to as *reverse bias*.

The theory of a p-n junction is more straightforward than that of a metal-semiconductor junction, because the role of the boundary states introduces an additional complexity which is absent in a p-n junction, where the charge on one side of the barrier is predominated by ionized donor im-

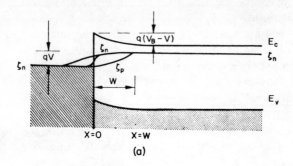

(a)

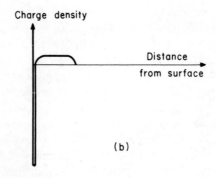

(b)

FIG. 20.3. (a) Electron energy band diagram for a metal-semiconductor barrier with forward bias. [From Gossick (1963).] (b) Charge density plotted against distance for a metal-semiconductor barrier with forward bias.

purities and the charge on the opposite side is predominated by ionized acceptor impurities so that both sides of the barrier may be accorded the same treatment.

The equilibrium barrier height V_B of a p-n junction depends upon the equilibrium concentration of conduction electrons on one side as compared with the other, or the equilibrium concentration of holes on one side as compared with the other. If the material is nondegenerate on both

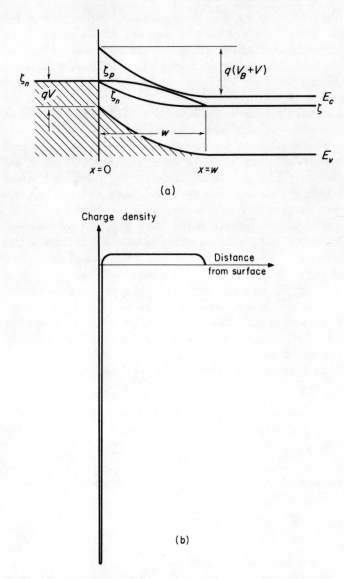

FIG. 20.4. (a) Electron energy band diagram for a metal-semiconductor barrier with reverse bias. (b) Charge density plotted against distance for a metal-semiconductor barrier with reverse bias.

sides of the barrier, then the Boltzmann relation between the equilibrium concentration of carriers on one side of the barrier, as compared with the other, gives the equilibrium barrier height. As the equilibrium concentration of minority carriers is inversely proportional to the equilibrium concentration of majority carriers, $n_0 p_0 = n_i^2$, it follows that the maximum barrier height is obtained with a high density of impurities on both sides of the barrier.

The width w of the barrier also depends upon the concentration of impurities. In order to charge the barrier capacitance sufficiently to accommodate the equilibrium barrier height, the boundaries of the space charge region must move back farther to expose an adequate number of impurities with relatively pure material than with impure material. Therefore, the conditions which produce a high barrier also produce a thin barrier. In order to obtain a high barrier and at the same time a wide barrier, one may make one side of the barrier rich in impurities of one type and the opposite side of the barrier lean in impurities of the opposite type. Obviously, a thin barrier will be subject to avalanche, or tunnel effects at a lower reverse voltage than a thick barrier. For this reason, barriers which are expected to rectify at large values of ac voltage are made with high resistivity material.

Exercise

(2.1) Derive the following expressions for the equilibrium barrier height V_B:

$$V_B = \frac{\kappa T}{q} \ln \left(N_{A-}\right)\left(N_{D+}\right)/n_i^2, \qquad \text{p-n junction}$$

$$V_B = \frac{\kappa T}{q} \ln N_{D+}p(0)/n_i^2, \qquad \text{metal semiconducting contact}$$

For the p-n junction (see Fig. 21.1a),

(a) let n_n and p_n denote the concentrations of electrons and holes respectively on the n side of the junction ($x_n < x$)

and p_p and n_p the concentrations of holes and electrons on the p side $(x < -x_p)$, and

(b) assume the n side of the junction to have a uniform concentration of ionized donors N_{D+} and the p side a uniform concentration of ionized acceptors N_{A-}, and that the conditions for the exhaustion temperature range apply, i.e., $N_{D+} = n_n$ and $N_{A-} = p_p$.

For the metal-semiconductor contact (see Fig. 20.2a),

(a) let n_0 and p_0 denote the equilibrium concentrations of electrons and holes, respectively, in the neutral semiconductor $(w < x)$, and

(b) assume the semiconductor to have a uniform concentration of ionized donors N_{D+}, and that the conditions for the exhaustion temperature range apply, i.e., $N_{D+} = n_0$.

Hint: Recall the relations

$$n_n p_n = N_{D+} p_n = n_i{}^2 = n_p p_p = N_{A-} n_p$$

2.1. Schottky Model of a Semiconductor Barrier

2.1.1. Potential Distribution in a Metal-Semiconductor Barrier (Planar and Hemispherical)

The Schottky model provides a method for estimating the field and potential within a barrier under certain conditions. The model was designed originally for metal-semiconductor rectifiers and will be discussed for the case of a metal n-type semiconductor barrier, and, in the following section, for a p-n junction rectifier. The Schottky model is described by the following six statements, two of which are redundant.

(I) The equilibrium barrier height V_B Fig. 20.2a is large compared with $\kappa T/q$.

(II) The barrier width w, Fig. 20.2a, is large compared with the Debye length based on the donor concentration.

(III) The electron concentration on the semiconductor side of the barrier is so large with respect to the hole concentration that it may be considered constant, i.e., $n(w) = N_{D+}$. Hence, the separation between conduction band and electrochemical potential of electrons remains constant over the range $w \leqq x$. Otherwise, the electrochemical potential of electrons may be adjusted to suit the conditions required by current flow and charging of boundary states. This latitude exists, as long as it is possible to neglect n and p in the determination of φ_i within the region $0 < x < w$.

(IV) The uncompensated ionized donor impurities in the potential barrier have a density

$$N_{D+}(x) = N_{D+} = \text{const}, \qquad 0 < x < w$$

$$= 0, \qquad\qquad w < x < L$$

and N_{D+} equals the equilibrium concentration of electrons n_0 at $x = w$.

(V) The charge density in the barrier is dominated by uncompensated ionized donor impurities, and therefore the following relations hold:

$$\int_0^w p \, dx \ll N_{D+}w \gg \int_0^w n \, dx$$

(VI) The hole concentration at the metal-semiconductor interface $p(0)$ does not exceed N_{D+}, i.e., $p(0) \lesseqgtr N_{D+}$.

The potential within a planar barrier is given by the solution of Poisson's equation,

$$d^2\varphi_i/dx^2 = -qN_{D+}/\epsilon, \qquad 0 < x < w \quad (211.1)$$

subject to the boundary conditions:

$$d\varphi_i/dx = 0, \qquad\qquad x = w \qquad (211.2a)$$

$$\varphi_i(w) = V_B - V, \qquad x = w \qquad (211.2b)$$

in which the potential at the interface has been set equal to zero, e.g., $\varphi_i(0) = 0$. The following relation defines the Debye length based on the donor concentration, mentioned in statement (II):

$$L_D{}^2 = \epsilon \kappa T / (q^2 N_{D+}) \qquad (211.3)$$

By integrating (211.1) once, and applying the boundary condition (211.2a), the following expression for the electric field in the barrier is obtained:

$$E(x) = \frac{(x - w)}{L_D} \frac{\kappa T}{q L_D}, \qquad 0 < x < w \qquad (211.4)$$

If (211.4) is integrated, and the boundary condition (211.2b) is applied, the result is the potential

$$\varphi_i(x) = \frac{w^2 - (w - x)^2}{2 L_D{}^2} \left(\frac{\kappa T}{q} \right), \qquad 0 < x < w \qquad (211.5)$$

with

$$\left(\frac{w}{L_D} \right)^2 \frac{\kappa T}{2q} = V_B - V \qquad (211.6)$$

Granting statement (I), it follows from (211.6) that statement (II) is true with reverse bias, and moderate forward bias.

The charge per unit area trapped in boundary states at $x = 0$ may be written

$$Q_s(V) = q N_{D+} w(V) \qquad (211.7)$$

with

$$w(V) = L_D \sqrt{2q(V_B - V)/\kappa T} \qquad (211.8)$$

The specific barrier capacitance, capacitance per unit area, is given by the following derivative of (211.7):

$$C_s = \frac{dQ_s}{dV} = \frac{\epsilon \sqrt{\kappa T}}{L_D \sqrt{2q(V_B - V)}} \qquad (211.9)$$

$$= \epsilon / w(V) \qquad (211.10)$$

Exercises

(2.2) Assuming the variation of φ_n to be slight within the barrier, and by expressing n through (211.5), obtain the following result:

$$\frac{1}{N_{D+}w}\int_0^w n\,dx = \frac{\sqrt{\pi}L_D}{\sqrt{2}w}\,\text{erf}\,\frac{w}{\sqrt{2}L_D}$$

and comment on to what extent it supports statement (V).

(2.3) Assuming the variation of φ_p to be slight within the barrier, and by expressing p through (211.5), obtain the following result:

$$\frac{1}{N_{D+}w}\int_0^w p\,dx = \left(\frac{L_D}{w}\right)^2 \frac{p(0)}{N_{D+}}$$

and discuss the conditions under which this result supports statement (V).

(2.4) Give an argument for elimination of the redundant statements, viz., (II) and (V).

Consider a hemispherical metal contact to a semiconductor, with radius r_1 defining the interface, corresponding to $x = 0$ in the planar case, and a radius r_2 defining the boundary of the space charge layer, corresponding to $x = w$ in the planar case. The barrier potential is given by the solution of Poisson's equation

$$\frac{1}{r^2}\frac{d}{dr}\left(r^2\frac{d\varphi_i}{dr}\right) = -\frac{qN_{D+}}{\epsilon}, \qquad r_1 < r < r_2 \quad (211.11)$$

subject to the boundary conditions

$$d\varphi_i/dr = 0, \qquad\qquad r = r_2 \qquad (211.12a)$$

$$\varphi_i(r_2) = V_B - V, \qquad r = r_2 \qquad (211.12b)$$

in which the potential at the interface has been set equal to zero, e.g., $\varphi_i(r_1) = 0$. If (211.11) is integrated and the boundary condition (211.12a) is applied, the result is the electric field

$$E(r) = \frac{\kappa T}{3qL_D{}^2}\left(r - \frac{r_2{}^3}{r^2}\right), \qquad r_1 < r < r_2 \quad (211.13)$$

The integration of (211.13) over r to r_2, with the boundary condition (211.12b), yields the potential

$$\varphi_i(r) = V_B - V - \frac{\kappa T}{3qL_D{}^2}\left[\frac{r_2{}^3}{r} + \frac{r^2}{2} - \frac{3r_2{}^2}{2}\right],$$

$$r_1 < r < r_2 \quad (211.14)$$

From the charge within the hemispherical barrier layer, which may be written purely through consideration of the geometry as

$$Q = \frac{2\pi}{3}qN_{D+}(r_2{}^3 - r_1{}^3) \qquad (211.15)$$

and the solution at the interface

$$\varphi_i(r_1) = 0 = V_B - V - \frac{\kappa T}{3qL_D{}^2}\left[\frac{r_2{}^3}{r_1} + \frac{r_1{}^2}{2} - \frac{3r_2{}^2}{2}\right] \quad (211.16)$$

the barrier capacitance

$$C_B = \left|\frac{dr_2}{dV}\right|\left|\frac{dQ}{dr_2}\right| \qquad (211.17)$$

may be obtained from the derivatives of (211.15) and (211.16), viz.,

$$C_B = \left|\frac{dQ}{dV}\right| = \frac{2\pi\epsilon r_1 r_2}{r_2 - r_1} \qquad (211.18)$$

There are two limiting cases: (1) r_2 is scarcely greater than r_1, and (2) r_2 is very much greater than r_1. Case (1) corresponds to a planar barrier for which the capacitance may be written

$$C_B = \frac{2\pi\epsilon r_1{}^2}{r_2 - r_1} \qquad (211.19)$$

while case (2) corresponds to a conducting hemisphere in a dielectric medium of permittivity ϵ with a capacitance

$$C_B = 2\pi\epsilon r_1 \qquad (211.20)$$

It might appear difficult to realize case (2) in practical examples, as r_1 could not exceed a few hundred angstroms. However, a metal-semiconductor boundary may have effective contact at the interface only at isolated points, making the effective capacitance of the barrier the sum of the capacitance of all points of contact, each of which would follow (211.20). The capacitance of such a contact should be relatively voltage independent over a moderate range of reverse bias.

The potential about the contact may also depend on the second spherical harmonic (Gossick, 1960), and it may be shown that the capacitance corresponding to this term also reduces to (211.20) for case (2).

2.1.2. Potential Distribution in a *p-n* Junction

Figure 21.1a shows the energy band diagram of a *p-n* junction in equilibrium, and Fig. 21.1b shows the energy band diagram of the same *p-n* junction with forward bias. Of the statements covering the metal-semiconductor rectifier, (I), (III), (IV), and (VI), we retain (I) without change, but modify the others as follows:

(III) Both the *p*-type and *n*-type regions are in the exhaustion range for the operative temperature, and the electron concentration on the *n*-side of the potential barrier is so large with respect to the hole concentration that it may be considered constant, i.e., $n(x_n) = N_{D+}$; and the hole concentration on the *p* side of the barrier is so large with respect to the *n* concentration that it may be considered constant, i.e., $p(-x_p) = N_{A-}$. Hence the electrochemical potential for electrons is fixed at $x = x_n$, and the electrochemical potential for holes is fixed at $x = x_p$. Otherwise the electrochemical potentials are free so that they may be adjusted to conform with the requirements of current flow.

(IV) The uncompensated ionized impurities in the planar barrier have the following density functions:

$$N_{A-}(x) = 0, \qquad\qquad\qquad x < -x_p$$
$$\phantom{N_{A-}(x)} = N_{A-} = \text{const}, \qquad -x_p < x < 0$$
$$\phantom{N_{A-}(x)} = 0, \qquad\qquad\qquad 0 < x$$
$$N_{D+}(x) = 0, \qquad\qquad\qquad x < 0$$
$$\phantom{N_{D+}(x)} = N_{D+} = \text{const}, \qquad 0 < x < x_n$$
$$\phantom{N_{D+}(x)} = 0, \qquad\qquad\qquad x_n < x$$

and

$$p(-x_p) = N_{A-},$$
$$n(x_n) = N_{D+},$$

(VI) The hole and electron concentrations at the inter-. face between n-type and p-type material satisfy the relations

$$n(0) \leqq N_{A-}, \qquad p(0) \leqq N_{D+}$$

The potential within the planar barrier is obtained by solving Poisson's equation

$$\frac{d^2\varphi_i}{dx^2} = -qN_{D+}/\epsilon, \qquad 0 < x < x_n$$
$$\phantom{\frac{d^2\varphi_i}{dx^2}} = qN_{A-}/\epsilon, \qquad -x_p \ll x < 0$$

(212.1)

subject to the boundary conditions

$$\frac{d\varphi_i}{dx} = 0, \qquad x = -x_p, x_n \quad (212.2a)$$

$$\varphi_i(x_n) - \varphi_i(-x_p) = V_B - V \qquad (212.2b)$$

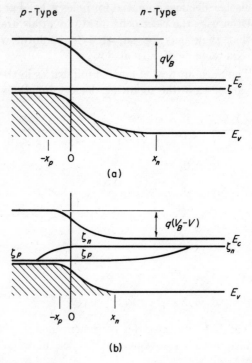

FIG. 21.1. (a) Electron energy band diagram for a p-n junction in equilibrium; (b) Electron energy band diagram for a p-n junction with forward bias.

and letting the potential equal zero at $x = 0$. The electric field is obtained by integrating (212.1) and applying boundary condition (212.2a):

$$E(x) = \frac{qN_{D+}}{\epsilon}(x - x_n), \qquad 0 < x < x_n$$

$$= -\frac{qN_{A-}}{\epsilon}(x + x_p), \qquad -x_p < x < 0 \qquad (212.3)$$

The potential is obtained by integrating (212.3) and applying boundary condition (212.2b):

$$\varphi_i(x) = \frac{qN_{D+}}{2\epsilon}[x_n{}^2 - (x_n - x)^2], \qquad 0 < x < x_n$$

$$= \frac{qN_{A-}}{2\epsilon}[(x_p + x)^2 - x_p{}^2], \qquad -x_p < x < 0 \quad (212.4)$$

Exercises

(2.5) Show that the barrier width, $w(V) = x_p + x_n$ is given by (211.8), if the concentration N_{D+} is replaced by the *reduced concentration*

$$N_{A-}N_{D+}/(N_{A-} + N_{D+})$$

which reduces to N_{D+} as N_{A-} becomes very large.

(2.6) Show that the specific barrier capacitance C_s is given by (211.10) with the concentration N_{D+} replaced by the *reduced concentration*.

(2.7) Show that if N_{D+} is either large or small compared with N_{A-}, then the validity of statement (VI), which implies that the following relations be satisfied:

$$\int_{-x_p}^{0} p \, dx \ll N_{A-}x_p \gg \int_{-x_p}^{0} n \, dx$$

and (or)

$$\int_{0}^{x_n} n \, dx \ll N_{D+}x_n \gg \int_{0}^{x_n} p \, dx$$

can hold only with appreciable reverse bias.

It would appear from Exercise (2.7) that the dependence of barrier capacitance on applied bias might not follow (211.9) for metal-semiconductor barriers with $[E_c(w) - \zeta] > [\zeta - E_v(0)]$ at equilibrium, or for alloy *p-n* junctions with $[E_c(x_n) - \zeta] > [\zeta - E_v(-x_p)]$ at equilibrium.

However, for reasons which are not at once obvious, the agreement between measurements and (211.9) is normally good with alloy and metal-plated junctions fabricated on uniform semiconductor pellets, not only with reverse bias, but with only moderate disagreement with forward bias.†

The reason for this apparent discrepancy is that the integral for specific charge in the barrier for establishing the field at the interface $x = 0$, is not the same as for the barrier capacitance. For example, the electric field at $x = 0$, with metal-semiconducting rectifiers, is given by the specific charge

$$\epsilon\left(\frac{d\varphi_i}{dx}\right)_{x=0} = q\int_0^w (N_{D+} + p - n)\,dx \qquad (212.5)$$

$$= q\Omega(V) \qquad (212.6)$$

with $\Omega(V)$ the number of occupied boundary states per unit area at $x = 0$, and with $p - n$ junctions

$$\epsilon\left(\frac{d\varphi_i}{dx}\right)_{x=0} = q\int_0^{x_n} (N_{D+} + p - n)\,dx \qquad (212.7)$$

$$= \int_{-x_p}^0 (N_{A-} + n - p)\,dx \qquad (212.8)$$

We may manipulate (212.5) and (212.6) to obtain

$$Q_s(V) = q[\Omega(V) - \int_0^w p\,dx] = q\int_0^w (N_{D+} - n)\,dx \quad (212.9)$$

and, by using the definitions of functions $N_{D+}(x)$ and $N_{A-}(x)$ given in statement (IV), we may obtain corresponding relations from (212.7) and (212.8), viz.,

$$Q_s(V) = q\int_{-x_p}^{x_n} [N_{A-}(x) - p]\,dx = q\int_{-x_p}^{x_n} [N_{D+}(x) - n]\,dx$$

$$(212.10)$$

---

† The author is indebted to Dr. R. Schwarz for the important elements of the following argument.

The specific charge Q_s, as given by (212.9) and (212.10), is appropriate for the barrier capacitance, as the charging current on the right side of the barrier consists of electron flow out of, or into, the space charge region, varying the integral $q \int_0^w (N_{D+} - n)\, dx$ in (212.9) for metal-semiconductor barriers and the integral $q \int_{-x_p}^{x_n} [N_{D+}(x) - n]\, dx$ in (212.10) in p-n junctions; and the charging current on the left side of the barrier consists of hole flow out of, or into, the space charge region, varying the integral

$$q \int_{-x_p}^{x_n} [N_{A-}(x) - p]\, dx$$

in (212.10) for p-n junctions, and, in addition to the flow of holes, a flow of electrons from the metal into surface states, varying the expression $q[\Omega(V) - \int_0^w p\, dx]$ in (212.9) with metal-semiconductor barriers. A detailed treatment of this subject, with experimental examples has been given by Schwarz and Walsh (1953).

Exercises

(2.8) Using the Schottky potentials in the expression for $p = n_i \exp q(\varphi_p - \varphi_i)/kT$ and $n = n_i \exp q(\varphi_i - \varphi_n)/kT$, and assuming φ_n and φ_p to remain almost constant, show that the integrals,

$$\frac{1}{N_{D+}w} \int_0^w (N_{D+} - n)\, dx, \quad \text{and} \quad \frac{1}{N_{D+}x_n} \int_{-x_p}^{x_n} [N_{D+}(x) - n]\, dx$$

remain near unity, even under conditions for which the Schottky model provides a very poor approximation.

(2.9) Using the results of Exercise (2.8), construct arguments which show that (211.9) gives a good approximation of the voltage dependence of barrier capacitance with reverse bias and a fair approximation with moderate forward bias for a junction either alloyed or plated on a pellet with high resistivity, and with an equilibrium barrier height exceeding half the band gap.

2.2. Bethe Model of a Semiconductor Barrier

The following model for a rectifying potential barrier within a semiconductor was originally presented by Bethe (1942) in an unpublished report written during World War II. The interface is pictured as an insulating layer of thickness δ, separating the metal from the semiconductor, as shown in Fig. 22.1. This picture is particularly applicable to

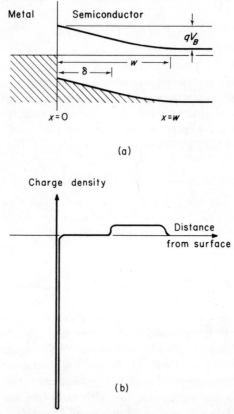

(a)

(b)

FIG. 22.1. (a) Electron energy band diagram for a metal-semiconductor barrier, conforming to the Bethe model, in equilibrium. (b) Charge density plotted against distance.

semiconducting oxide, in which case a thin layer of the pure insulating oxide may be deliberately prepared over the semiconducting oxide before the metal contact is applied, or the process of applying the metal contact may automatically produce such an insulating layer. The abrupt transition between the insulating and semiconducting oxide is, of course, an over simplification. The simplicity of the model permits an easy solution, which illustrates the effect of placing an insulating layer between a metal contact and a semiconductor, and from which the electrical characteristics may be conveniently interpreted.

Poisson's equation takes the following form for a planar barrier:

$$\frac{d^2\varphi_i}{dx^2} = 0, \qquad\qquad 0 < x < \delta \qquad (220.1)$$

for the part of the barrier occupied by an insulator, and

$$= -qN_{D+}/\epsilon, \qquad \delta < x < w \qquad (220.2)$$

for the part occupied by a uniform semiconductor with ionized donor concentration N_{D+}, which also extends beyond the barrier $(w < x)$. As before, the potential at the interface $x = 0$ is taken to be 0. The potential within the barrier is the solution of Poisson's equation subject to the following boundary conditions:

$$\varphi_i(w) = V_B - V \qquad\qquad (220.3)$$

$$(d\varphi_i/dx)_{x=w} = 0 \qquad\qquad (220.4)$$

with the potential and field continuous at $x = \delta$. That solution may be written as follows:

$$\varphi_i(x) = \frac{qN_{D+}}{\epsilon}(w - a)x, \qquad\qquad 0 < x < \delta \qquad (220.5)$$

$$= \frac{qN_{D+}}{2\epsilon}\{w^2 - \delta^2 - (w - x)^2\}, \quad \delta < x < w \qquad (220.6)$$

The Bethe model gives the following width for the barrier:

$$w^2 = \delta^2 + \frac{2qL_D^2}{\kappa T}(V_B - V), \qquad \delta \leqq w \quad (220.7)$$

As with the Schottky model, the electrons and holes are neglected in the space charge within the barrier, and the charge per unit area which enters into the barrier capacitance may be written

$$Q_s = qN_{D+}(w - \delta) \qquad (220.8)$$

The following expression for the barrier capacitance per unit area comes from Eqs. (220.7) and (220.8):

$$C_s = \frac{dQ_s}{dV} = \frac{\epsilon}{w} = \frac{\epsilon}{\sqrt{\delta^2 + \dfrac{2qL_D^2}{\kappa T}(V_B - V)}} \qquad (220.9)$$

The conditions of the problem as stated in Poisson's equation make its solution physically valid only for values of the barrier width w equal to, or greater than, the thickness of the insulating layer δ, or for applied voltage V less than or equal to, the equilibrium barrier height V_B. Therefore, we must reconsider the problem under a different set of conditions for applied voltage exceeding the equilibrium barrier height. With V exceeding V_B, the following statements apply:

(1) There is no mechanism for further reduction of w and it remains constant at $w = 0$.

(2) The electric field at the interface between the metal contact and insulating layer $E(0)$ becomes positive and increases in magnitude with increasing bias.

(3) The current is space charge limited as V exceeds V_B.

The capacitance per unit area has been plotted in terms of the square of its reciprocal against applied voltage in Fig. 22.2. This linear plot should provide a convenient graphical means of determining the thickness of the insulating layer δ through the intercept of the decreasing linear function

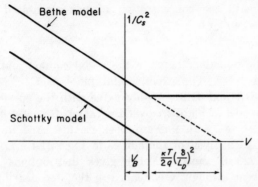

FIG. 22.2. Barrier capacitance per unit area for the Bethe and Schottky models, plotted in terms of the square of reciprocal capacitance against applied voltage.

and the voltage axis. For applied voltage exceeding the equilibrium barrier height, the barrier should behave as an ordinary capacitance with a dielectric layer of thickness δ. However, the diffusion of charge carriers into and beyond the barrier does not attain the condition of steady flow until a certain lapse of time, and this effect can coincide with the charging time of the barrier in such a way as to make the measured capacitance fall either below or above the constant value indicated in Fig. 22.2 for values of applied voltage exceeding the equilibrium barrier height. The time dependence of the conduction current as opposed to the charging current is treated later in Sections 3.1.1 and 3.1.2.

English and Gossick (1964) have investigated the capacitance of gold-rutile barriers. They estimated the distribution of ionized donors throughout the space charge layer by analyzing the measured barrier capacitance according to a method given originally by Schottky (1942) and employed subsequently by Rath (1956), which utilizes the relation

$$\frac{2}{\epsilon q}\frac{dV}{dC_s^{-2}} = N_{D+}(x) \qquad (220.10)$$

to estimate the concentration of uncompensated ionized donors at a depth

$$x = \epsilon/C_s \qquad (220.11)$$

from the boundary between the metal contact and the insulating layer. The experimental plots of C_s^{-2} versus V (Figs. 31.1 and 31.2) roughly agree with the curve for the Bethe model in Fig. 22.2 over the range of reverse bias (the measurements with forward bias are discussed in Section 3.1.1). An analysis of the curves in Figs. 31.1 and 31.2 by Eqs. (220.10) and (220.11) gives distributions $N_{D+}(x)$ which bear a rough resemblance to the step distribution of the Bethe model.

With applied voltage substantially exceeding the magnitude of the equilibrium barrier height, the current should be space charge limited, and, according to the simple model treated by Mott and Gurney (1948), the current should increase as the square of the applied voltage, as indicated by the expression

$$J_n = \frac{9\mu\epsilon V^2}{8\delta^3} \qquad (220.12)$$

Perhaps it should be mentioned that (220.12) is based on oversimplified conditions, so that it yields only rough agreement in most instances. Detailed models for space charge limited current in semiconductors have been reported by Lampert (1959, 1961), and by Lindmayer and Slobodskoy (1963).

Measurements of the forward current-voltage characteristics of metal-ceramic rutile rectifiers are shown in Fig. 22.3 (English and Gossick, 1964). The measurements were made with periodic current pulses of short duration compared with the period to prevent overheating. The values of voltage indicated in Fig. 22.3 refer to the voltage applied across the barrier, as a correction has been made in each case for the voltage drop in the semiconducting substrate in series with the rectifying barrier. It may be seen that the

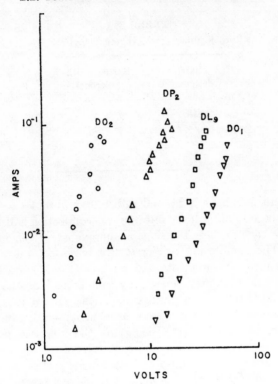

F<small>IG</small>. 22.3. Logarithm of forward current versus logarithm of voltage applied across the barrier, measured with a pulse generator (0°C). [From English and Gossick (1964).]

logarithm of the current is approximately a linear function of the logarithm of the applied voltage. The barrier DP_2 with the donor distribution most like that of the Bethe model (as indicated by capacitance measurements) yields a slope of approximately two in Fig. 22.3, showing a small increase in slope at large voltage which suggests the presence of trapping states (Lampert, 1962). The barrier DO_1 with the donor distribution more like the Bethe model, except for DP_2, yields a slope of approximately two, but shows a more definite increase in slope than DP_2 at large voltage. Barriers

TABLE 20.1

EQUILIBRIUM BARRIER WIDTHS

Barrier designation	Barrier width (microns)
DO_2	1.6
DP_2	3.9
DL_9	4.9
DO_1	7.5

DO_2 and DL_9 have a gradual rather than abrupt transition from the insulating layer into the semiconducting substrate, and for each of these the slope is approximately four in Fig. 22.3. The equilibrium barrier widths w, as determined by capacitance measurements and relation (220.11) are listed in Table 20.1. It may be seen, by comparing Fig. 22.3 with Table 20.1, that, for a given voltage, the current is greater the thinner the barrier. The measurements which exhibit a pronounced scatter were made on the thinnest barrier (DO_2), and, with this test specimen, the voltage drop across the series resistance comprised such a large part of the total applied voltage that it was difficult to make a precise determination of the part applied across the barrier.

CHAPTER 3

Rectification
by a Barrier Layer

3.0. Physical Processes of Semiconductor Rectifiers

Consider a p-n junction in equilibrium,[†] which would correspond to the band energy diagram in Fig. 21.1a. As the system is in equilibrium there is no net current flow. However, it is clear that there will be a partial flow of electrons from left to right, as electrons on the left which are within a diffusion length of the edge of the potential barrier will diffuse to the barrier and fall downhill, gain energy crossing the barrier, and in this way pass from the p-type to the n-type region. It is assumed here that we have a planar barrier in which the p-type material extends to the left of the barrier well beyond a diffusion length $\sqrt{D_n \tau_n}$. The current density of this component of electron flow may be determined as follows. The current density is given by the product of the electronic charge q times the equilibrium electron density on the p side, n_{p0}, times the diffusion velocity which by (125.15) equals $\sqrt{D_n/\tau_n}$, e.g.,

$$J_{ns} = q n_{p0} \sqrt{D_n/\tau_n} \qquad (300.1)$$

Those electrons on the n side which have enough energy to surmount the barrier and flow into the p side have a density $n_{n0} \exp(-q V_B/\kappa T)$, through the Boltzmann relation, and this density must equal n_{p0} by (102.1). As the net current vanishes, the electron current density into the p side must match that into the n side, as given by (300.1). Therefore, as the charge and electron density are the same in both cases, the transport velocity of electrons into the p side

---

[†] The theory of the rectification process of a p-n junction was stated originally by Shockley (1949).

must also be the diffusion velocity $\sqrt{D_n/\tau_n}$ as indicated by (300.1). The current density of electrons which flows in opposite directions at equilibrium, given by (300.1), is called the *saturation current density of electrons*. Certain features of this case were previously treated implicitly in the derivation of the Einstein relation between the mobility and diffusion coefficient (Section 1.0.3). An analogous argument may be applied to the saturation current density of holes, on which basis one may write the following expression for the components of hole current density which flow equally in both directions at equilibrium

$$J_{ps} = qp_{n0}\sqrt{D_p/\tau_p} \qquad (300.2)$$

When forward bias is applied, the Fermi level is no longer the same on both sides of the junction, but varies from one side to the other, and splits throughout the barrier and surrounding transition region into separate electrochemical potentials, one for electrons and one for holes, Fig. 21.1b. There is now a greater abundance of electrons on the n-side of the barrier with sufficient energy to surmount the barrier and pass over to the p-type region. The concentration of these electrons has been increased by the Boltzmann factor $\exp(qV/\kappa T)$. However, the concentration of electrons on the p-side, which diffuses to the barrier and falls downhill into the n-side remains unchanged. The difference of the two components gives the electron current density, as expressed by the following relation (Wagner, 1931):

$$J_n(V) = J_{ns}[\exp(qV/\kappa T) - 1] \qquad (300.3)$$

An analogous argument may be given to show that the current density of holes may be written

$$J_p(V) = J_{ps}[\exp(qV/\kappa T) - 1] \qquad (300.4)$$

A qualitative explanation for the dependence of the electrochemical potentials on distance (Fig. 21.1b) is briefly outlined. The flow of electrons from the n side to the p side produces an excess of electron concentration near the barrier in the p-type region. As the electrons diffuse further into the

p-type material, they recombine with holes, and the concentration of electrons diminishes until it reaches the equilibrium value. This decrease in the concentration of electrons with distance from the barrier is indicated by the decrease in the electrochemical potential ζ_n with distance from the barrier, and the excess electron concentration vanishes where ζ_n has merged with ζ_p into a single value. There should be a slight slope to the electrochemical potential within the barrier to account for the flow of electrons across the barrier through relation (113.10). An analogous account could be given for the variation in the electrochemical potential for holes ζ_p. The slope of the electrochemical potential for electrons, on the left of the barrier, is steeper than the slope of the electrochemical potential for holes, on the right of the barrier, indicating that the decay rate of electrons in the p-type region is greater than that of holes on the n side.

With reverse voltage, the number of electrons on the n side with sufficient energy to surmount the barrier is less than under equilibrium conditions, and the component of flow from left to right is partially uncompensated. With sufficient reverse bias, virtually no flow of electrons takes place from right to left, and the current flow becomes saturated at the value J_{ns}. It is for this reason that the quantities J_{ns} and J_{ps} are referred to as the saturation current density of electrons, and the saturation current density of holes, respectively.

The mechanism for rectification of a metal-semiconductor rectifier is similar to that of a p-n junction.† At equilibrium the electrons with sufficient energy to cross the barrier are in the same concentration on both sides, as the concentration for that energy depends only on the separation of the energy from the Fermi level. As the electrons pass from the boundary of the barrier into the metal they become degraded in energy. Whereas electrons, injected into the p side of a p-n junction,

---

† The theoretical model of a metal-semiconductor rectifier presented here is after Schultz (1954) as far as holes are concerned, but for electrons, it is original with the author (1963).

lose energy through single transitions across the forbidden energy gap through the recombination process, the electrons injected into the metal from a metal-semiconductor junction lose a little more energy than the amount of the equilibrium barrier potential through collisions with phonons in the metal.

Two different electrochemical potentials for electrons in the metal are indicated in Fig. 20.3. One decreases gradually, while the other decreases abruptly to the value of ζ_n for the bulk metal. The curve which decreases abruptly corresponds to the electrochemical potential of all conduction electrons in the metal, as customarily defined. The curve which decreases gradually is the electrochemical potential of only the electrons, which have energy exceeding ζ_n for the bulk metal. It is in the latter special sense that we apply the electrochemical potential of electrons in metals throughout the remainder of the text. To account for the distribution in energy of the excess electrons in the region near the barrier the electrochemical potential of the excess electrons slopes gradually downward as it passes into the metal. This transition of the electrochemical potential may take place over a distance of several thousand angstroms.

The population of unoccupied states below the Fermi level in the metal is normally high enough to maintain the concentration of holes practically constant at the metal-semiconductor interface regardless of applied bias (Swanson, 1954). Therefore, with forward bias, holes are injected from the barrier layer into the n-type side on the right in about the same manner as with a p-n junction.

Both the historical and theoretical development of models for semiconductor rectification have been treated by Henisch (1957).

3.0.1. Diode and Diffusion Theories Related to Majority Carriers (dc Current)

A phenomenological model for injecting electrons from a semiconductor through a potential barrier into a metal is presented, which gives the contribution to the rectifying characteristics by the electrons (Gossick, 1963).

The conduction electrons in the metal are crudely separated into two populations:

(I) the "hot electrons," with energy exceeding a threshold value E_l, and with initial energy when injected into the metal, exceeding an upper threshold value E_h and

(II) the "cool electrons," with energy below the threshold value E_l.

The term "hot" is sometimes applied to electrons in the metal whose energy is 5 to 10 volts over the Fermi surface, but the term "hot" is restricted here to electrons which are only comparatively warm with the threshold energy E_h no more than 1.5 volts over the Fermi surface and in many cases not more than $\frac{1}{2}$ volt above the Fermi surface.

The concentration of cool electrons is always very large compared with that of hot electrons. The hot electrons decay to cool electrons through a relaxation process with an attenuation time τ_m, and attenuation length $L_m = \sqrt{D_m \tau_m}$, with D_m the diffusion coefficient of hot electrons in the metal. Hence, the hot electrons in a metal play an analogous role to conduction electrons in a p-type semiconductor. Generalizing from the analog, the population of hot electrons is treated as a Fermi gas obeying the classical approximation, with the extension to the nonequilibrium case treated by replacing the Fermi level ζ by the electrochemical potential ζ_n. The following expression for the attenuation length may be derived on the basis of kinetic theory, using the same argument that gives the "Fermi age" of pile neutrons, viz.,

$$L_m = \lambda_m \sqrt{\nu/3} \tag{301.1}$$

with λ_m the mean free path of hot electrons and ν the mean number of collisions required to convert a hot electron to a cool electron. It follows from the Bohm–Pines (1953) theory that the restriction on the threshold energy E_h makes the electron-phonon scattering dominate over electron-electron scattering in the relaxation process. The mean free path of hot electrons, which is inherently less than the mean free path which enters into the electrical conductivity of the bulk metal, may be written $1/\lambda_m = 1/\lambda_{me} + 1/\lambda_{mf}$ in which λ_{me} the electron-electron mean free path is normally greater than λ_{mf} the electron-phonon mean free path. Under favorable conditions, typified by gold-germanium contacts, $E_h - E_l$ will be less than 0.7 eV and $\lambda_m = \lambda_{mf}$, and the number ν may be estimated by the following expression, based on the theory of hot electrons (Koenig, 1959):

$$\nu = \frac{\ln(E_h/E_l)}{\ln[1 - (4m_m{}^*c_s{}^2/\kappa T)]} \tag{301.2}$$

in which c_s denotes the velocity of sound in the metal, and $m_m{}^*$ the effective mass of hot electrons.

A one-dimensional solution follows which gives the electron flow, through a planar barrier. The coordinate x gives the distance from the metal-semiconductor interface, with positive values applying to depth into the semiconductor and negative values for depth into the metal (Fig. 20.2a). It is assumed that both the metal and the semiconductor are uniform, and that the latter has a constant concentration of ionized donor impurities.

We reject the IR drop which appears across the semiconductor outside the barrier, by defining the applied voltage V as that part which appears only across the barrier. As the current density of hot electrons decreases with increasing separation from the barrier, the current density of cool electrons must correspondingly increase to maintain a non-divergent total current density everywhere in the metal. This requirement is met by a drift current density of cool electrons produced by a small potential difference within the metal which is negligible compared with that applied across the barrier. Therefore, the metal is taken to be a short circuit, as compared with the semiconductor, making the potential constant throughout the metal, and the density of

hot electrons within the metal depends only on the electrochemical potential $\zeta_n(x)$, $x < 0$ (Fig. 20.3a). The constant
value of potential in the range $x < 0$ is taken as zero. Only
barriers which have a height $E_c(0) - E_c(w)$ much greater
than κT are considered. It is assumed that the thickness of
the metal layer is much greater than the attenuation length
L_m. The threshold energy values, which define hot and cool
electrons, and determine the collision number ν are assigned
as follows: E_h equals $E_c(0)$ the energy of the bottom of the
conduction band of the semiconductor at the interface $x = 0$,
and E_l equals ζ the equilibrium Fermi level.†

The concentration of hot electrons in the metal is written

$$n(x) = n \exp[\zeta_n(x)/\kappa T], \qquad x < 0 \qquad (301.3)$$

and the concentration of conduction electrons in the barrier
is written

$$n(x) = n_i \exp\{[\zeta_n(x) + q\varphi_i(x)]/\kappa T\}, \qquad 0 < x < w$$

$$(301.4)$$

The following expression gives the current density of hot
electrons in the metal:

$$J_n(x) = \frac{qD_m n(x)}{\kappa T} \frac{d\zeta_n}{dx}, \qquad x < 0 \qquad (301.5)$$

The electronic charge is denoted by q. Only hot electrons are
transported across the interface, $x = 0$. Hence, at that interface, Eq. (301.5) gives the total current density of electrons.
The current density in the barrier, $0 < x < w$, is given by
(301.5) with D_m replaced by the diffusion coefficient of conduction electrons in the semiconducting barrier D_n. Assuming
recombination to be negligible within the barrier, the dc

---

† Actually, E_l should exceed ζ by κT, but as it has been implicitly
assumed that $(E_h - E_l) \gg \kappa T$, the error introduced by simply taking
ζ for E_l is quite small.

current density satisfies the following continuity relations:

$$-\frac{1}{q}\frac{dJ_n}{dx} + \frac{n(x) - n_i e^{\zeta/\kappa T}}{\tau_m} = 0, \qquad x < 0 \qquad (301.6)$$

$$-\frac{1}{q}\frac{dJ_n}{dx} = 0, \qquad 0 < x < w \quad (301.7)$$

subject to the boundary conditions: both $J_n(x)$ and $\zeta_n(x) - \zeta$ continuous across the interface, $x = 0$ and $\zeta_n(x) - \zeta = qV$ at the edge of the space charge layer, $x = w$. The solution of (301.6)

$$\exp\left(\frac{\zeta_n(x) - \zeta}{\kappa T}\right) - 1 = \left\{\exp\left(\frac{\zeta_n(0) - \zeta}{\kappa T}\right) - 1\right\}\exp\left(\frac{x}{L_m}\right),$$

$$x < 0 \quad (301.8)$$

which provides the following current density at the interface:

$$J_n(0) = J_{ms}\{\exp([\zeta_n(0) - \zeta]/\kappa T) - 1\} \quad (301.9)$$

with

$$J_{ms} = [qD_m n_i \exp(\zeta/\kappa T)]/L_m \qquad (301.10)$$

Consider the special case of a "thin" barrier, with a width of the order of the mean free path λ. According to an argument accompanying Fig. 11.2, the conduction electrons can gain energy $-qV$ when a potential V is applied over a distance of the order of a mean free path or less. Hence, the concentration of conduction electrons at the interface, $x = 0$, is multiplied by a factor $\exp qV/\kappa T$, but this factor may also be written in general as $\exp[\zeta_n(0) - \zeta]/\kappa T$, recalling that $\varphi_0(0) = 0$. Then, recalling also that recombination was initially assumed to be negligible in the barrier so that we may write $J_n(x) = J_n(V)$, $0 < x < w$, and replacing the term $\exp[\zeta_n(0) - \zeta]/\kappa T$ in (301.9) by $\exp(qV/\kappa T)$, that relation gives us another Wagner equation [see (300.3) and (300.4)]

$$J_n(V) = J_{ms}\{\exp(qV/\kappa T) - 1\} \qquad (301.11)$$

with J_{ms} the saturation current density of electrons given by (301.10). There is an older argument known as the "diode" theory which yields a solution $\sqrt{3\nu}/4$ times relation (301.11).

We turn now to a "thick barrier" $(w \gg \lambda_n)$, which may still be thin compared with $\sqrt{D_p\tau_p}$, the diffusion length for holes. With germanium and silicon $\sqrt{D_p\tau_p}$ may be $(10)^4$ times λ_n which provides sufficient latitude for the barrier width w to meet the requirement $\lambda_n \ll w \ll \sqrt{D_p\tau_p}$. Therefore, we are permitted to retain the initial assumption that recombination may be neglected even in a "thick" barrier.

The integration of (301.7) over the barrier gives the following constant:

$$J_n(0) = qD_n n_i \exp(q\varphi_i/\kappa T)\frac{d \exp[\zeta_n(x)/\kappa T]}{dx},$$

$$0 < x < w \quad (301.12)$$

which may be rearranged and integrated again over the barrier to yield

$$\exp[\zeta_n(0)/\kappa T] = \exp[\zeta_n(w)/\kappa T]$$

$$- \frac{J_n(0)}{qD_n n_i}\int_0^w \exp(-q\varphi_i/\kappa T)\ dx \quad (301.13)$$

By the boundary conditions, $J_n(0)$ in (301.12) and $J_n(0)$ in (301.13) are equal and may be replaced by $J_n(V)$. The terms $\exp[\zeta_n(0)/\kappa T]$ in (301.9) and (301.13) are equal according to the boundary conditions, and are eliminated by substituting (301.13) for $\exp[\zeta_n(0)/\kappa T]$ in (301.9). If the last step is followed by replacing $\zeta_n(w) - \zeta$ by qV, the result is the following expression for the current density:

$$J_n(V) = \frac{J_{ms}[\exp(qV/\kappa T) - 1]}{\left\{1 + \int_0^w \exp(-q\varphi_i/\kappa T)\ dx[D_m/(D_n L_m)]\right\}}$$

$$(301.14)$$

The major contribution to the integral

$$\int_0^w \exp(-q\varphi_i/\kappa T)\ dx$$

in the denominator of (301.14) is made over a small part of the range near zero. Therefore, a reasonable approximation may be obtained by replacing φ_i by its first term $-E_0 x$ with $E_0 = -d\varphi_i/dx$, $x = 0$, which gives for the integral

$$\int_0^w \{\exp(qE_0 x/\kappa T)\}\ dx = \{\exp(qE_0 w/\kappa T) - 1\}\kappa T/(qE_0)$$

$$(301.15)$$

As the field at the interface, E_0, is negative, and the energy barrier $E_c(0) - E_c(w)$ is large compared with κT, then the integral (301.15) reduces to the simple expression $(\kappa T/qE_0)$ which may be substituted in (301.14) to give the following result:

$$J_n(V) = J_{ms}[\exp(qV/\kappa T) - 1]\left(1 + \frac{D_m \kappa T}{D_n L_m q\ |\ E_0\ |}\right)^{-1}$$

$$(301.16)$$

If the term $(D_m \kappa T)(D_n L_m q\ |\ E_0\ |)^{-1}$ in the denominator of (301.16) is large compared with unity, then (301.16) reduces to the following well known result of Schottky (1939) and Mott (1939), based on diffusion theory:

$$J_n(V) = q\mu_n\ |\ E_0\ |\ n_i \exp(\zeta/\kappa T)[\exp(qV/\kappa T) - 1]$$

$$(301.17)$$

However, if the term $(D_m \kappa T)(D_n L_m q\ |\ E_0\ |)^{-1}$ is small compared with unity, then (301.16) reduces to (301.11) which was derived for a "thin" barrier. Let us consider the magnitude of the ratio

$$(D_m \kappa T)(D_n L_m q\ |\ E_0\ |)^{-1}$$

$$= (\kappa T/q\lambda_n\ |\ E_0\ |)(3m_n{}^*)^{1/2}(\nu m_m{}^*)^{-1/2} \quad (301.18)$$

which determines whether a rectifying barrier is "thin" or "thick," i.e., whether (301.16) favors (301.11) or (301.17). The symbol m_n^* denotes the effective mass of electrons in the semiconducting barrier, and λ_n the mean free path of conduction electrons in the barrier, which is taken somewhat smaller than in the bulk semiconductor in order to account for the reflection coefficient at the interface for each individual electron, an effect otherwise neglected in the derivation of (301.14). Two classes of metal-semiconductor barriers are considered, one which employs germanium, silicon, or one of the III–V compounds with electrical properties similar to germanium, e.g., GaAs, and the other which employs an oxide semiconductor such as the rutile structure of TiO_2.

In the first class, $m_n^* \sim m_m^*$ with metals normally used for contacts, and $\nu \sim 5$ to 8, which makes the factor $(3m_n^*)^{1/2}(\nu m_m^*)^{-1/2}$ of the order of 0.1 or 1.0. The Schottky field (211.4) gives a reasonable estimate of $|E_0|$, and with this substituted in the factor $(\kappa T)(q\lambda_n \,|\, E_0 \,|)^{-1}$ in (301.18), it becomes $(w\kappa T)(2q\lambda_n V_B)^{-1}$ with zero bias. We take as reasonable values, $V_B \sim 0.3$ to 0.6 volt, $\lambda_n \sim 600$ Å, and $w \sim 10,000$ to 15,000 Å, and find that the ratio (301.18) can be expected to be of the order 0.1 or 1.0 with zero bias. The conclusion is that some rectifying barriers of the first class (Si, Ge, GaAs, etc.) can be expected to conform approximately to (301.11) over a modest range of applied voltage, and this conclusion is supported by the experimental literature. However, with many of these rectifiers, the ratio (301.18) in the denominator of (301.16) is neither small nor large compared with unity, with the result that the current-voltage characteristics fall between the limiting cases (301.11) and (301.17).

In the second class, the mass m_n^* may be an order of magnitude or so larger than m_m^*, because the conduction electrons in an oxide semiconductor may employ a narrow energy band derived from the d shell, which makes for a large effective mass as explained in connection with (101.44), and with $\nu \sim 5$ to 8, the factor $(3m_n^*)^{1/2}(\nu m_m^*)^{-1/2}$ may be of the order

1.0 or 10. Estimating the field $|E_0|$ from the Bethe model for zero bias gives $(\delta \kappa T)(\lambda_n q V_B)^{-1}$ as a rough approximation of the factor $(\kappa T)(q\lambda_n|E_0|)^{-1}$ in (301.18). Although the barrier height V_B may exceed $\kappa T/q$ by from one to two orders of magnitude, the electronic mean free path in oxides may be so small as to make δ four orders of magnitude greater than λ_n. Hence, the ratio (301.18) should be sufficiently large to make (301.16) reduce to the expression for current density of "thick" barriers (301.17), for the second class (e.g., TiO_2).

Although the most pronounced dependence of (301.17) on applied voltage V is on the factor $[\exp(qV/\kappa T)-1]$, there is a dependence on V through the factor $|E_0|$. The field at the interface $|E_0|$ may be approximated by the Schottky model, through relations (211.4) and (211.8), as

$$|E_0| = [2qN_{D+}(V_B - V)\epsilon^{-1}]^{1/2} \qquad (301.19)$$

and by the Bethe model, through (220.7) with $(w - \delta) \ll w$, as

$$|E_0| = (V_B - V)/\delta \qquad (301.20)$$

The influence of (301.19) and (301.20) is to make the forward current increase less, and the reverse current more, than indicated by the factor

$$[\exp(qV/\kappa T) - 1]$$

with increasing forward and reverse voltage, respectively; and from the practical viewpoint of rectification this influence is, of course, undesirable.

Some explanatory remarks are in order related to the variation in the effective mass of the electrons as a function of the location within the barrier, and the reflection coefficient of the electrons at the interface, $x = 0$, on the basis of quantum mechanics. Equation (301.12) was obtained by the integration of (301.7) over the barrier. This integration implicitly takes into account the variation of the effective mass as a function of x. Hence, the diffusion coefficient D_n, in which the effective mass enters, is an average over the region $0 < x < w$. Therefore D_n in (301.12)–(301.14) differs from its value for the bulk semiconductor. In practical cases, the equilibrium barrier thickness of germanium is at least an order of magnitude greater than the electronic mean free path. The barrier thickness compared with the mean free path is proportionately greater with silicon than germanium, and with titanium dioxide rectifiers the barrier thickness is several orders of magnitude greater than the mean free path. Therefore the conduction electrons which traverse the barrier suffer many collisions in transit. Some electron scattering occurs at the interface boundary, which, when added to the scattering by phonons and ionized impurities, should make the mean free path which enters in the diffusion coefficient D_n smaller than in the bulk semiconductor. To determine D_n for a particular case, it must be considered in terms of the band structure and potential variation within the barrier for that case.

Exercises

(3.1) Consider the hemispherical contact delineated in Section 2.1.1, and add the restriction that $L_m \gg r_1$. Take several practical examples, and solve for r_2. Note that r_2 is never large compared with r_1.

(3.2) Continuing with the hemispherical contact of the previous exercise, derive the expression for the current as a function of the applied voltage. Show that the current is approximately $2\pi r_1^2$ times the current density in the planar case (301.14), as long as the restriction $L_m \gg r_1$ is retained.

3.0.2. Rectification by Minority Carriers (dc Current)

The contribution of holes to the current density through a planar metal-semiconductor barrier $J_p(V)$ under an applied voltage V, will be determined next.† Some of the applicable

---

† The discussion in Section 3.0.2 is also applicable to p-n junctions fabricated to make the p-type region very impure compared with the n-type region.

conditions to this problem will be stated directly. Similar conditions have been stated in previous sections, and are restated here for convenience, and also in order to point out their particular relation to the properties of holes.

(I) The metal provides a short circuit for conduction electrons, and a sufficient supply of unoccupied electronic states to maintain a constant hole concentration $p(0)$ at the metal-semiconductor interface.

(II) The IR drop in the region $w < x < L_0$ is small compared with the voltage applied to the potential barrier.

(III) The barrier width w is small compared with the diffusion length of holes L_p.

(IV) The hole concentration is always small compared with the electron concentration in the region $w < x < L_0$.

It follows from (I) that the metal has a negligible effect in limiting hole current, and also that

$$p(0) = p_0 \exp qV_B/\kappa T \qquad (302.1)$$

One may conclude from (II) that the concentration of holes in the region $w < x < L_0$ depends only on the electrochemical potential $\zeta_p(x)$. It may be stated, as a corollary to (III), that recombination may be neglected within the potential barrier, making $J_p(0) = J_p(w)$. Hence, it will suffice to determine $J_p(w)$, and it will be justified to write it as $J_p(V)$. It follows from (IV) that we may consider the difference $(E_c(x) - \zeta_n(x)]$ to be equivalent to the equilibrium value $(E_c - \zeta)$ in the range $w < x < L_0$.

It follows from the conditions and corollaries just stated, together with (125.18) and (126.4), that the current density of holes may be written

$$J_p(V) = \frac{qD_p}{L_p}[p(w) - p_0], \qquad L_0 \gg L_p \quad (302.2)$$

and

$$J_p(V) = \frac{qD_p}{L_0 - w}[p(w) - p_0], \qquad L_0 \ll L_p \quad (302.3)$$

for a thick and thin base, respectively. If we make an approximation based on condition (IV), formerly discussed in connection with (125.2), then we may write $[p(w) - p_0]$ as $p_0[\exp qV/\kappa T - 1]$ in (302.2) and (302.3) and obtain the Wagner equation

$$J_p(V) = J_{ps}[\exp qV/\kappa T - 1] \qquad (302.4)$$

with the saturation current density

$$J_{ps} = qp_0 D_p/L_p \qquad (302.2a)$$

for a thick base, and

$$J_{ps} = qp_0 D_p(L_0 - w)^{-1} \qquad (302.3a)$$

for a thin base. A more accurate solution may be obtained by solving for $[p(w) - p_0]$ rather than evaluating it by relation (125.2). As the current density is constant in the region $0 < x < w$, through condition (III), we may write

$$J_p(V) = -qD_p\left(\frac{dp}{dx} + \frac{qp}{\kappa T}\frac{d\varphi_i}{dx}\right) \qquad (302.4)$$

or

$$J_p(V) = -qD_p\left[\exp(-q\varphi_i/\kappa T)\frac{d}{dx}\exp(q\varphi_i/\kappa T)\right]p \quad (302.5)$$

Rearranging (302.5) and performing an integration over the barrier leads to the expression

$$[p(w) - p_0] = p_0[\exp(qV/\kappa T) - 1]$$

$$- \frac{J_p(V)}{qD_p}\exp[-q(V_B - V)/\kappa T]\left[\int_0^w \exp(q\varphi_i/\kappa T)\,dx\right]$$

$$(302.6)$$

Inserting (302.2) and (302.3), respectively, into (302.6) reduces the latter to

$$[p(w) - p_0]$$

$$= \frac{p_0[\exp(qV/\kappa T) - 1]}{1 + \exp[-q(V_B - V)/\kappa T]\int_0^w \exp(q\varphi_i/\kappa T)\,dx/L_p}$$

$$(302.7)$$

for a thick base, and

$$[p(w) - p_0]$$

$$= \frac{p_0\exp(qV/\kappa T) - 1}{1 + \exp[-q(V_B - V)/\kappa T]\int_0^w \exp(q\varphi_i/\kappa T)\,dx/(L_0 - w)}$$

$$(302.8)$$

for a thin base. As the integral in the denominators of (302.7) and (302.8) is related only to the region $0 < x < w$, and therefore has nothing to do in either case with whether the base is thin or thick, the distinguishing features of the correction term in the denominator of $[p(w) - p_0]$ are the factors L_p^{-1} in (302.7) and $(L_0 - w)^{-1}$ in (302.8), and as $(L_0 - w) \ll L_p$ the correction term should be much more significant with the thin base.

It remains to evaluate the integral

$$\int_0^w \{\exp q[\varphi_i - (V_B - V)]/\kappa T\}\,dx$$

in (302.7) and (302.8). The major contribution to that integral comes in the region near $x = w$. Therefore, we may obtain a reasonable approximation of the integral by replacing φ_i by its second order expansion about the point $x = w$, e.g.,

$$\varphi_i(x) = V_B - V - \varphi_{iw}''(x - w)^2/2 \qquad (302.9)$$

with

$$\varphi_{iw}'' = \left| \frac{d^2\varphi_i}{dx^2} \right|_{x=w}$$

which makes the integral reduce to

$$\int_0^w \exp\left(\frac{q[\varphi_i - (V_B - V)]}{\kappa T} \right) dx = \frac{\sqrt{\pi\kappa T}}{\sqrt{2q\varphi_{iw}''}} \operatorname{erf} \frac{w\sqrt{q\varphi_{iw}''}}{\sqrt{2\kappa T}}$$

$$(302.10)$$

Near $x = 0$ the Schottky potential is most inaccurate, because the concentration of holes (neglected in the Schottky model) is highest, but the contribution to (302.10) in this region is slight. On the other hand, the Schottky potential is a good approximation of $\varphi_i(x)$ near $x = w$, the region which makes the largest contribution to the integral. Therefore, a reasonable approximation of the integral may be obtained by replacing (302.9) by (211.5), which gives for the integral

$$\int_0^w \exp\left(\frac{q[\varphi_i - (V_B - V)]}{\kappa T} \right) dx = \frac{\sqrt{\pi}}{\sqrt{2}} L_D \operatorname{erf} \frac{w}{\sqrt{2}L_D} \quad (302.11)$$

which may be rewritten through (211.6) as

$$\int_0^w \exp\left(\frac{q[\varphi_i - (V_B - V)]}{\kappa T} \right) dx = \frac{\sqrt{\pi}}{\sqrt{2}} L_D \operatorname{erf} \frac{q(V_B - V)}{\kappa T}$$

$$(302.12)$$

Therefore, by combining relations (302.2), (302.7) and (302.3), (302.8), respectively, with (302.12) we have the approximation of the hole current density:

$$J_p(V) = \frac{q D_p p_0 [\exp(qV/\kappa T) - 1]}{L_p + \frac{\sqrt{\pi}}{\sqrt{2}} L_D \operatorname{erf} \frac{q(V_B - V)}{\kappa T}} \quad (302.13)$$

for a thick base, and

$$J_p(V) = \frac{q D_p p_0 [\exp(q V / \kappa T) - 1]}{L_0 - w + \frac{\sqrt{\pi}}{\sqrt{2}} L_D \operatorname{erf} \frac{q(V_B - V)}{\kappa T}} \qquad (302.14)$$

for a thin base. With germanium or silicon having long life-time, L_p may be orders of magnitude greater than L_D, making (302.13) reduce to

$$J_p(V) = \frac{q D_p p_0}{L_p} [\exp(q V / \kappa T) - 1] \qquad (302.15)$$

for the thick base. Otherwise, the term involving the error function in the denominators of (302.13) and (302.14) cannot be neglected. It should be emphasized that neither (302.13) nor (302.14) can hold with appreciable forward bias, because of the restriction imposed by condition (IV).

Exercises

(3.3) Show that the ratio of hole to electron current through a metal-semiconductor barrier, i.e., the injection ratio γ (312.10) may be approximated in the exhaustion temperature range, over a modest range of applied voltage, by the expression

$$\gamma = \frac{J_p}{J_n} = \left(\frac{D_p L_m}{D_m L_p} \right) \frac{p(0)}{N_{D+}}$$

for the "diode" theory, and

$$\gamma = \frac{J_p}{J_n} = \frac{D}{L_p \mu_n \mid E_0 \mid} \frac{p(0)}{N_{D+}}$$

for the "diffusion" theory.

(3.4) Refer to Exercise (2.3) and note that if $p(0) \leqq N_{D+}$, then the Schottky model is reasonably accurate. Taking typical values of D_m and L_m for gold, and D_p and L_p for germanium, show that the hole current is normally smaller than the electron current if the Schottky model is reasonably accurate.

(3.5) Take the hemispherical contact considered in Exercise (3.1), and keep the restrictions imposed on the relative magnitudes of the radii r_1 and r_2. Verify that the hole current through the hemisperical contact is given by the expression

$$I_p = \frac{2\pi r_2 q D_p p_0 [\exp(qV/\kappa T) - 1]}{1 + r_2 \exp[-q(V_B - V)/\kappa T] \int_{r_1}^{r_2} \exp(q\varphi_i/\kappa T) \, dr/r^2}$$

(3.6) Construct an argument to illustrate that with an oxide with large forbidden energy gap (e.g. TiO_2, rutile, with approximately 3.1 eV for the gap) the potential barrier, at an interface with a metal contact, may still be high compared with κT, and, at the same time, sufficiently small compared with the gap to make $p(0) \ll N_{D+}$. Hence, with metal-rutile barriers, the majority carriers should not only dominate ($\gamma \ll 1$), but behave according to the diffusion theory.

(3.7) Assuming such quantities as the diffusion length and diffusion coefficient of minority carriers and the equilibrium concentration of majority carriers to be fixed, show that the saturation current of minority carriers decreases sharply with increasing forbidden gap.

The discussion of the nonequilibrium characteristics of a semiconductor potential barrier under steady current flow is concluded here. Special cases were selected to illustrate the fundamental physical processes of semiconductor rectifiers. A more general treatment becomes lengthy and complicated. However, as only length and complexity are introduced rather than new principles, a suitable background has been provided for the extensive literature. Van Roosbroeck (1950) and Saby (1956) among others have treated large excess carrier concentrations. The behavior of semiconductor rectifiers with large reverse bias voltage has been completely neglected here. It is a separate field in itself which has been treated comprehensively elsewhere by Shotov (1958), Shockley (1961), and Chynoweth (1960).

As experimental studies of the behavior of metal-semiconductor rectifiers and p-n junctions abound in the journals of applied physics and electrical engineering, there is therefore justification for including only a few experimental studies here. The primary purpose of this monograph is to summarize some of the simple theoretical models which apply to semiconductor rectifying barriers. It should be pointed out that the agreement between the simple rectifying equations and experimental behavior is generally poor, but this is not necessarily a reflection on the theoretical models for the following reason. The fabrication of semiconducting rectifiers is a complicated technological art. Inadequate control of the atmosphere, uniformity and purity of materials, the temperature and various other conditions of the fabrication process can yield rectifiers which do not correspond to simple mathematical models. Junctions between the n-type and p-type regions that were designed to be planar may instead have protuberances pointing in any direction. The edge effects which are omitted in the one dimensional solution for a planar barrier are only negligible with germanium and silicon rectifiers, providing the surfaces have been etched and otherwise properly treated. It seems safe to say that each major theoretical model has been ultimately confirmed by a breakthrough in the art of fabrication, a case in point being the tunnel model. The first theoretical model of semiconductor rectification, Wilson (1932), Nordheim (1932), and by Frenkel and Joffe (1932), was finally confirmed after a quarter of a century by Esaki (1958) who was the first to succeed in making tunnel diodes.

The remainder of this text is devoted to the non-equilibrium characteristics of semiconductor rectifying barriers under application of applied voltage which varies with time. The transient behavior of semiconductor rectifiers may be treated from two points of view. It may be treated so as to predict the behavior of semiconductor rectifying barriers in practical electronic circuits, or it may be treated in a theoretically restricted sense so as to provide more insight into the physical processes related to semiconductor rectifiers. The latter point of view underlies the treatment which follows.

3.1. The Time Dependent Behavior of Semiconductor Rectifiers

3.1.1. Alternating Current by Majority Carriers

The electron current through a planar metal-semiconductor rectifier, as treated in Section 3.0.1 for direct current is extended here to alternating current. By replacing φ_i in (301.4) by the first order term $-E_0 x$ and repeating the derivation in Section 3.0.1, the result summarized by (301.16) is obtained. Therefore, by replacing (301.4) with the expression

$$n(x) = n_i \exp[\zeta_n(x) - qE_0 x]/\kappa T, \qquad 0 < x < w \quad (311.1)$$

which is done hereafter, the results will have an accuracy comparable to expression (301.16).

When an oscillating term is superimposed on the electron density, the continuity relations (301.6) and (301.7) may be written

$$-i\omega[n(x) - n_i e^{\zeta/\kappa T}] = -\frac{1}{q}\frac{dJ_n}{dx} + \frac{n(x) - n_i e^{\zeta/\kappa T}}{\tau_m},$$
$$x < 0 \qquad (311.2)$$

in the metal, and

$$-i\omega n = -\frac{1}{q}\frac{dJ_n}{dx}, \qquad 0 < x < w \quad (311.3)$$

in the potential barrier. Equations (311.2) and (311.3) reduce, respectively, to

$$\left[\frac{d^2}{dx^2} - \left(\frac{1}{L_m'}\right)^2\right]\left[\exp\left(\frac{\zeta_n(x) - \zeta}{\kappa T}\right) - 1\right] = 0, \quad x < 0 \quad (311.4)$$

with L_m' representing $L_m/\sqrt{1 + i\omega\tau_m}$, and

$$\left[\frac{d^2}{dx^2} - \frac{qE_0}{\kappa T}\frac{d}{dx} - \frac{i\omega}{D_n}\right]\exp\left(\frac{\zeta_n(x) - \zeta}{\kappa T}\right) = 0,$$

$$0 < x < w \quad (311.5)$$

As differential equations (311.4) and (311.5) are linear and homogenous, and the solutions are linear combinations, that with $\omega = 0$ applies to the dc case, while that with $\omega \neq 0$ gives an oscillation superimposed on the dc solution. Let the amplitude of the oscillating part of $\exp[\zeta_n(x) - \zeta]/\kappa T$ be denoted $\Gamma(x)$. Then, from (311.4) we have

$$\Gamma(x) = \Gamma(0)\epsilon^{x/L_m} \quad (311.6)$$

Let

$$d = -qE_0/2\kappa T \quad (311.7)$$

and

$$b = \sqrt{a^2 + i\omega/D_n} \quad (311.8)$$

and the solution of (311.5) may be written

$$\Gamma(x) = A\exp[-(d + b)x] + B\exp[-(d - b)x] \quad (311.9)$$

It follows from the definition of $\Gamma(x)$ that the following expressions give the amplitude of oscillating current density:

$$J_n'(x) = qD_mn_i\exp(\zeta/\kappa T)\frac{d\Gamma(x)}{dx},$$

$$x < 0 \quad (311.10)$$

$$J_n'(x) = qD_nn_i\exp\left(\frac{\zeta - qE_0x}{\kappa T}\right)\frac{d\Gamma(x)}{dx},$$

$$0 < x < w \quad (311.11)$$

The following matrix equation comes from (311.9)–(311.11) with application of the boundary conditions: $J_n'(x)$ and $\Gamma(x)$ continuous across the interface, $x = 0$, and

$$\Gamma(w) = [\exp(qV/\kappa T)]qV'/\kappa T \quad (311.12)$$

with applied voltage $V + V'e^{i\omega t}$ under the restriction $qV' \ll \kappa T$:

$$\begin{pmatrix} 1 & -J_{ms}' & -J_{ms}' \\ 1 & J_{sa}' & J_{sa}'' \\ 1 & e^{-(d+b)w} & e^{-(d-b)w} \end{pmatrix} \begin{pmatrix} J_n' \\ A \\ B \end{pmatrix} = \begin{pmatrix} 0 \\ 0 \\ \Gamma(w) \end{pmatrix}$$

(311.13)

with

$$J_{ms}' = J_{ms}\sqrt{1 + i\omega\tau_m}$$

$$J_{sa}' = (1 + b/d)q\mu_n \mid E_0 \mid n_i e^{\zeta/\kappa T}$$

$$J_{sa}'' = (1 - b/d)q\mu_n \mid E_0 \mid n_i e^{\zeta/\kappa T}$$

The symbol J_n' in (311.13) denotes the amplitude of ac electron current density, making the oscillating term $J_n'(t) = J_n'e^{i\omega t}$ which is given by the following solution of (311.13):

$$J_n'(t) = \frac{2q\mu_n b n_i V' \exp[(qV + \zeta)/\kappa T + i\omega t]}{P(w)} \quad (311.14)$$

with

$$P(w) = \left\{\left[1 + \frac{L_m'D_n(d + b)}{D_m}\right]\exp[-(d - b)w]\right.$$

$$\left. - \left[1 + \frac{L_m'D_n(d - b)}{D_m}\right]\exp[-(d + b)w]\right\} \quad (311.15)$$

With metal-semiconductor barriers in which the semiconductor is of the type Si, Ge, GaAs, etc., the time constants in (311.14) are so short compared with the time constants related to the diffusion and recombination of holes that J_n' may be fairly regarded as frequency independent. However, with oxide rectifiers (e.g., TiO_2), the band gap, barrier height, and donor density ordinarily stand in such relation as to make the electron current dominate the total current, so that the time constants connected with the hole current may be neglected [see Exercise (3.6)]. Making a suitable approximation of (311.14) for such cases, and taking into account the charging of the barrier capacitance $C_B(V)$, one has the following ac admittance of the barrier:

$$Y(i\omega) = i\omega C_B(V) + \left(\frac{dI}{dV}\right)_{dc} \exp\left[- \frac{i\omega\kappa Tw}{D_n q \mid E_0 \mid}\right] \quad (311.16)$$

with the dc barrier conductance $(dI/dV)_{dc}$ the derivative of dc current with respect to bias. The inductive effect of the second term in (311.16) should become pronounced with forward bias, given sufficient barrier width w. The voltage dependence of the first term on the left has already been discussed in Section 2.1 and it has been illustrated for two simple cases in Fig. 22.2. However, the measured capacitance also contains the imaginary part of the term on the right. The factor $(dI/dV)_{dc}$, the dc barrier conductance, is so small with reverse bias as to make the contribution of that term negligible, but that factor becomes sufficiently large with forward bias to make the term on the right come into play. That term is also voltage dependent, through the factor w in the exponent, but, in the range of forward bias where the term on the right makes a contribution, the voltage dependence of w is negligible compared with that of the factor $(dI/dV)_{dc}$.

With semiconducting oxide rectifying barriers, the inductive effect of the term on the right (311.16) may noticeably appear in the measured barrier capacitance. Measurements of the barrier capacitance of metal-ceramic rutile barriers (English and Gossick, 1964) are shown in Figs. 31.1 and 31.2; Fig. 22.3 and Table 20.1 also refer to the same rectifying barriers. With two of the four barriers, the measured capacitance decreases markedly with forward bias and the most plausible explanation for this dependence on bias would appear to be the inductive contribution of the term on the right (311.16). Although two of the ceramic rutile barriers

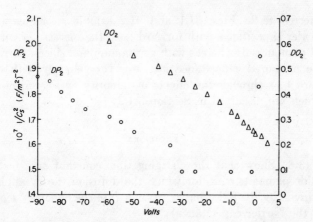

FIG. 31.1. Barrier capacitance per unit area (C_s) for diodes DO_2 and DP_2 measured at a temperature of 0°C, using a frequency of 100 kc/sec, plotted in terms of the square of the reciprocal specific capacitance against the voltage applied across the barrier (V). [From English and Gossick (1964).]

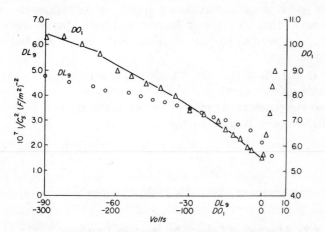

FIG. 31.2. Barrier capacitance per unit area (C_s) for diodes DL_9 and DO_1 measured at a temperature of 0°C, using a frequency of 100 kc/sec, plotted in terms of the square of the reciprocal specific capacitance against the voltage applied across the barrier (V). [From English and Gossick (1964).]

referred to in Figs. 31.1 and 31.2 exhibit an increase in barrier capacitance with forward bias, the increase is not at all pronounced; whereas with germanium and silicon barriers the measured capacitance increases very sharply with forward bias through the effects of minority carrier injection, which are discussed in Section 3.1.2.

Exercises

(3.8) Show that the charging time constant of a metal-oxide planar barrier, for which the diffusion theory applies, is given by the following expression (use the Schottky model of the barrier capacitance):

$$RC = \frac{\epsilon}{\sigma_n} \left[\frac{\kappa T \exp[q(V_B - V)/\kappa T]}{2q(V_B - V)} \right]$$

(3.9) Show that the charging time constant of a metal-oxide hemispherical barrier (as delineated in Section 2.1.1), for which the diffusion theory applies, is approximately the same as that of a planar barrier, as long as the restriction $L_m \gg r_1$ is retained (use the Schottky model of the barrier capacitance).

(3.10) Show that the charging time constant of a metal-oxide planar barrier, for which the diffusion theory applies, and the potential within the barrier is approximated by the Bethe model, is given by the expression

$$RC = \frac{\epsilon}{\sigma_n} \left\{ \frac{\kappa T \exp[q(V_B - V)/\kappa T]}{q(V_B - V)} \right\}$$

over the range of bias $-V_B < V < V_B$, $w \gg (w - \delta)$.

3.1.2. Alternating Current by Minority Carriers

The fluctuating component of hole current through a planar metal-semiconductor barrier under an applied voltage $V + V'e^{i\omega t}$ will be determined, subject to the four conditions stated at the beginning of Section 3.0.2.† In addition, the following condition is stipulated. The electrochemical potential for holes $\varphi_p(w)$, at the boundary of the potential barrier, $x = w$, is considered to remain at the equilibrium value φ. The addition of this condition incurs the loss in accuracy which results from dropping the second term in (302.6), but only to the extent that it influences one of two factors of the fluctuating component of the hole current, as will be noted later.

Consider the equations, stated in Section 1.2.5, for the current density (125.4) and the continuity equation (125.5) of holes in the region $w < x$. When an oscillating term is superimposed on the excess hole density, then, on the basis of (125.4) and (125.5), the excess concentration of holes may be written

$$-i\omega p_1 = -D_p \frac{d^2 p_1}{dx^2} + \frac{p_1}{\tau_p}, \qquad w < x < L_0 \quad (312.1)$$

or, after collecting terms,

$$\frac{d^2 p_1}{dx^2} - \left(\frac{1 + i\omega\tau_p}{D_p \tau_p}\right) p_1 = 0, \qquad w < x < L_0 \quad (312.2)$$

As (312.2) is the same as (125.6), with the diffusion length for holes L_p replaced by

$$L_p' = L_p / \sqrt{1 + i\omega\tau_p} \qquad (312.3)$$

then the solution of (312.2) is given by the solution of (125.6), i.e., (125.9) with $\sqrt{D_p\tau_p}$ replaced by (312.3), viz.,

$$p_1(x) = [p(w) - p_0] \exp[(w - x)/L_p'] \qquad (312.4)$$

and the density of hole current, given by (125.14), but restated as

$$J_p(x) = q p_1(x) D_p / L_p \qquad (312.5)$$

---

† The discussion in this section also applies to p-n junctions in which the p-type region is very impure compared with the n-type region.

for the dc case, gives the expression for the ac case with L_p replaced by (312.3). From condition (III), Section 3.0.2, we have $J_p(0) = J_p(w)$, and as the barrier width w is a function of applied voltage, we may write

$$J_p(V) = q p_1(w) D_p / L_p'$$ (312.6)

As differential equation (312.2) is linear and homogenous, and the solutions are linear combinations, that with $\omega = 0$ gives the dc term, and that with $\omega \neq 0$ gives the ac term of the excess hole concentration. Hence, with an applied voltage, $V + V' e^{i\omega t}$, under the restriction $qV' \ll \kappa T$, the ac value of $p_1(w)$ to be used in (312.6) may be expressed as

$$\left(\frac{q p_0 V'}{\kappa T} \right) \exp\left(\frac{qV}{\kappa T} + i\omega t \right)$$

and the ac term of hole current density as

$$J_p'(t) = (J_p)_{dc} \left(\frac{qV'}{\kappa T} \sqrt{1 + i\omega\tau_p} \right) e^{i\omega t}$$ (312.7)

The inaccuracy incurred by considering the electrochemical potential for holes at $x = w$ to remain at the equilibrium value may be confined to the factor $\sqrt{1 + i\omega\tau_p}$ in (312.7) by evaluating $(J_p)_{dc}$ by (302.13) the derivation of which was free of that condition.

The amplitude of the oscillating current density of electrons, $J_n' e^{i\omega t}$, given by (311.14) is practically frequency independent with germanium and silicon. Therefore, with rectifiers made of these materials, we may write for the total alternating current

$$J'(t) = \left[\frac{q(I_n)_{dc}}{\kappa T} + \frac{q(I_p)_{dc}}{\kappa T} \sqrt{1 + i\omega\tau_p} + i\omega C_B \right] V' e^{i\omega t}$$

(312.8)

This relation may also be stated in terms of the following

barrier admittance:

$$Y(i\omega) = \frac{q(I_n)_{dc}}{\kappa T} + \frac{q(I_p)_{dc}}{\kappa T}\sqrt{1 + i\omega\tau_p} + i\omega C_B \quad (312.9)$$

Use is sometimes made of the approximately constant ratio of the contributions to the direct current by holes and electrons, in terms of the injection ratio γ defined as

$$\gamma = \frac{I_{minority\ carriers}}{I_{majority\ carriers}}, \quad \text{for dc current} \quad (312.10)$$

Then, taking $(I)_{dc}$ as the total direct current, (312.9) may be rewritten as

$$Y(i\omega) = \frac{q(I)_{dc}}{\kappa T}\{1 - \gamma + \gamma\sqrt{1 + i\omega\tau_p}\} + i\omega C_B \quad (312.11)$$

According to the treatment of current density in this section, $q(I)_{dc}(\kappa T)^{-1}$ equals the barrier conductance, $(dI/dV)_{dc}$. Therefore, (312.11) may be rewritten as

$$Y(i\omega) = (dI/dV)_{dc}\{1 - \gamma + \gamma\sqrt{1 + i\omega\tau_p}\} + i\omega C_B$$

$$(312.12)$$

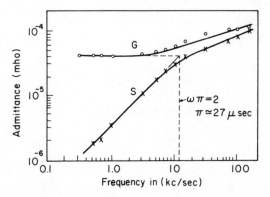

FIG. 31.3. Real and imaginary parts, G and S, of the admittance versus frequency curves. [From Kanai (1954).]

The use of relation (312.9) to determine the recombination time τ_p from measurements of the barrier admittance (Goucher *et al.*, 1951; Rath, 1956); Kanai, 1954), is illustrated in Fig. 31.3.

The modulation of the series resistance of the semiconducting material, beyond the boundaries of the potential barrier, through the injection of minority carriers constitutes an inductive impedance, the effects of which were observed by Yearian (1948) before the phenomenon of minority carrier injection was recognized. This effect was studied and reported later by Kanai (1955), Rath (1956), and in detail by Spenke (1958).

Exercise

(3.11) Consider a hemispherical barrier, as delineated in Section 2.1.1. Show that with a bias $V + V'e^{i\omega t}$, with $V' \ll \kappa T/q$, the fluctuating component of hole current is given by the expression

$$ J_p(t) = qp_0 D_p \left[\frac{1}{r_1} + \frac{1}{L_p'} \right] [\exp(qV/\kappa T) - 1] \frac{qV'}{\kappa T} e^{i\omega t} $$

3.1.3. Transient Characteristics

Studies of the transient behavior of semiconductor rectifiers may be conveniently classified according to the following categories:

(1) The small amplitude transient response, in which the departure of the barrier height from its equilibrium value is much less than $\kappa T/q$, i.e., $V \ll \kappa T/q$.

(2) The variation of applied voltage under a pulse of forward current, during which the barrier height departs from its equilibrium height by a large amount compared with $\kappa T/q$, i.e., $V \gg \kappa T/q$.

(3) The open-circuit voltage after a pulse of forward current ($V \gg \kappa T/q$).

(4) The reverse recovery current following a pulse of forward current $(V \gg \kappa T/q)$.

The small amplitude transient response, category (1), is of practical interest in connection with solid state particle detectors, Mayer (1959), Engler (1960), and is of interest also because it provides a clear picture of the separate roles played by the charging time of the potential barrier and the characteristic diffusion times of the charge carriers. Studies of the open-circuit voltage after a pulse of forward current, category (3), are of interest because they may be used to determine the equilibrium barrier height, and the recombination time of minority carriers (Gossick, 1953, 1955, 1956; Lederhandler and Giacoletto, 1955; Armstrong, 1956). The studies of applied voltage during and after a pulse of forward current, categories (2) and (4), are of practical interest because the rectifying barrier is unable to permit the full flow of forward current in response to the application of forward voltage until the minority carriers are injected, nor able to block the flow of reverse current in response to the application of reverse voltage until minority carriers are collected (Bray, 1949; Waltz, 1952; Bray and Gossick, 1953; Gossick, 1953; Pell, 1953; Shulman and McMahon, 1953; Steele, 1954; Lax and Neustadter, 1954; Barsukov, 1957; Ko, 1961).

The ac admittance for small amplitude current fluctuations superimposed upon the direct current has already been given for a metal-semiconducting oxide barrier (311.16) and for a minority carrier injecting metal-semiconductor barrier (312.9). As a treatment of the frequency domain is tantamount to a treatment of the time domain, through the generality of Fourier series and integrals, it follows that the ac admittance of the barrier may be used to determine its transient response (Gossick, 1955, 1956). The relation between the time dependent applied voltage and the current may be written in general in terms of Laplace transforms through the following relation:

$$V'(s) = I'(s)/Y(s) \tag{313.1}$$

taking

$$F'(s) = \int_0^\infty e^{-st}F(t)\,dt \tag{313.2}$$

as the definition of the Laplace transform of a function $F(t)$; $Y(s)$ in (313.1) is the barrier admittance with $i\omega$ replaced by s. It has been shown by James and Weiss (1947) that, given a linear relation (313.1) between current and voltage, the transient voltage $V(t)$ is related in general to an arbitrary current $I(t)$ through the following convolution integral:

$$V(t) = \int_0^t I(t-\lambda)f(\lambda)\,d\lambda \tag{313.3}$$

in which

$$f'(s) = 1/Y(s) \tag{313.4}$$

Equations (313.3) and (313.4) together illustrate that, once the ac admittance of the barrier has been determined, its transient behavior has been also, in principle, determined. Since the Laplace transform of a unit impulse current $\delta(t)$ is unity, then, by (313.1), the voltage response of the barrier, to a unit impulse current, is given by the inverse transform of the reciprocal of the barrier admittance, or, as indicated also by (313.3) and (313.4). The next expression, which gives the barrier voltage following a unit impulse current for a planar barrier has been derived from (313.3) and (313.4) using the admittance

$$Y(s) = (dI/dV)_{dc}\{1 - \gamma + \gamma\sqrt{1 + s\tau_p}\} + sC_B \tag{313.5}$$

which is given by (312.12) with $i\omega$ replaced by s,

$$f(t) = \frac{\exp(-t/\tau_p)}{(\xi + \chi)C_B}\{\xi \exp(\xi^2 t)\,\mathrm{erfc}\,-\xi\sqrt{t}$$
$$+\chi \exp(\chi^2 t)\,\mathrm{erfc}\,\chi\sqrt{t}\} \tag{313.6}$$

with

$$\xi = \left\{ \tau_p \left(\frac{\gamma}{2\Theta} \right)^2 + \frac{1}{\tau_p} - \frac{1 - \gamma}{\Theta} \right\}^{1/2} - \frac{\gamma \sqrt{\tau_p}}{2\Theta} \quad (313.7)$$

and

$$\chi = \xi + \frac{\gamma \sqrt{\tau_p}}{\Theta} \quad (313.8)$$

in which Θ denotes the charging time of the barrier $C_B (dI/dV)_{dc}^{-1}$. The initial value of (313.6) illustrates that an impulse current consists entirely of displacement current. The diffusion of holes enters the decay process after the impulse current charges the barrier, before the barrier has time to discharge through the barrier conductance $(dI/dV)_{dc}$. With unity injection ratio $(\gamma = 1)$, there are two limiting cases of particular interest. With reverse bias of sufficient magnitude, Θ becomes so much greater than τ_p that (313.6) reduces to

$$f(t) = \frac{\exp(-t/\Theta)}{C_B} \quad (313.9)$$

On the other hand, with a sufficient amount of forward bias, Θ becomes so much less than τ_p, that here (313.6) reduces to

$$f(t) = \frac{\exp[\tau_p t/\Theta^2] \, \mathrm{erfc} \, \sqrt{\tau_p t}/\Theta}{C_B} \quad (313.10)$$

Normally the time constants which apply to the mode of decay given by (313.9) are at least ten times as great as the characteristic decay time given by (313.10). Therefore, an applicable comparison of the two cases is afforded by the plots of $e^{-t/10}$ and $e^t \, \mathrm{erfc} \, \sqrt{t}$ shown in Fig. 31.4. The author has considered the solutions for the small amplitude transient behavior in detail elsewhere (Gossick, 1955, 1956; Curtis and Gossick, 1956).

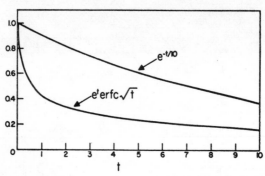

FIG. 31.4. Plots of the functions $e^{-t/10}$ and $e^t \operatorname{erfc} \sqrt{t}$. [From Gossick (1956).]

The transient decay of small excursions of the barrier voltage produced by a unit impulse current may be qualitatively summarized as follows. With reverse bias, minority carriers are not injected, and only the charging time of the barrier Θ enters into the transient barrier voltage. With low forward bias, the barrier capacitance discharge time permits the diffusion of holes beyond the barrier. The diffusion of holes then enters the recovery time, and the voltage decay assumes forms of the error function which are characteristic of diffusion processes (313.10). The recovery time decreases with forward bias through the bias dependence of Θ in (313.10). As the discharge time of the space-charge region Θ decreases with increasing forward bias, less time is available for holes to diffuse beyond the barrier. Therefore, the collection time for holes and the barrier discharge time decrease together with increasing forward bias.

Figure 31.5 shows a typical test circuit for studying the open-circuit decay voltage $V(t)$ following an injection current of long duration in the forward direction. The operation of the test circuit may be briefly described as follows: the test diode is shown on the right, and it is connected to the pulse generator on the left through a fast-recovery diode whose recovery time is very short compared with that of the

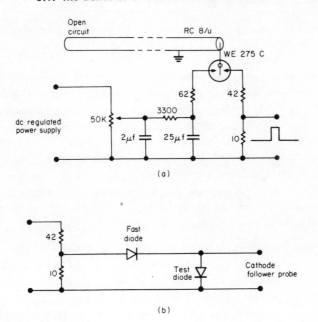

FIG. 31.5. (a) Pulser circuit. (b) Test circuit for measuring transient behavior of rectifiers.

test diode. The voltage across the test diode is detected by a cathode-follower probe and displayed on an oscilloscope screen as a function of time. During the injection of forward current, the fast-recovery diode acts almost as a short circuit, but, after the injecting pulse, it resembles an open circuit.

The barrier capacitance is ordinarily charged to a voltage which is initially large enough to satisfy the inequality $V(0) \gg \kappa T/q$. With metal-germanium rectifying barriers, the RC time constant is normally brief compared with the recombination time of injected holes throughout the range of forward voltage. Consequently, the discharge time can not limit the recovery process, and may be ignored. The recovery time then depends only on the diffusion and re-combination of the excess holes. However, with a wider forbidden gap, as with metal-silicon rectifying barriers, the conductance $(dI/dV)_{dc}$ becomes sufficiently small with decreasing forward bias to make the barrier RC discharge time enter into and prolong the recovery. Furthermore, with metal-semiconducting oxide barriers, such as gold-ceramic rutile rectifiers, the current is carried predominantly by the majority carriers and the recombination process scarcely enters into the transient behavior, with the result that the recovery is completely dependent upon the discharge of the barrier capacitance.

Consider a germanium alloyed planar p-n junction, with barrier width w, as shown schematically in Fig. 12.5, for which the following conditions apply.

(I) The n-type region is uniform over the range, $w < x < L_0$, and of very high resistivity as compared with that of the p-type alloyed material on the left of the barrier. Under these conditions, when the barrier capacitance is charged, the maximum variation in the quasi-Fermi level of holes $\Delta\zeta_p(t)$, $x = w$, has the magnitude of $qV(t)$, with $V(t)$ the amount by which the barrier has been reduced below its equilibrium height (see Fig. 31.6). Hence, the voltage $V(t)$ depends on the excess hole concentration through the relations

$$p(w, t) = p_0 \exp \Delta\zeta_p(t)/\kappa T \qquad (313.11)$$

$$p(w, t) = p_0 \exp qV(t)/\kappa T \qquad (313.12)$$

and

$$p_1(w, t) = p(w, t) - p_0 = p_0\Xi(t) \qquad (313.13)$$

with

$$\Xi(t) = \exp(qV(t)/\kappa T) - 1 \qquad (313.14)$$

(II) The excess hole concentration at the boundary of the region on the right $(x = L_0)$ vanishes

$$p_1(L_0, t) = 0 \qquad (313.15)$$

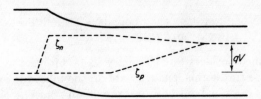

Fig. 31.6. Energy band diagram of a p-n junction, switched to open circuit after a large injection of forward current.

(III) The initial excess hole concentration is given by the relation

$$p_1(x, 0) = p_0 \Xi(0) \exp(w - x)/L_1 \qquad (313.16)$$

with $L_1 \ll L_0$. With injection time long compared with the lifetime τ_p, and modest voltage $V(0)$, it follows from (125.10) that L_1 equals the diffusion length $\sqrt{D_p \tau_p}$, but, with brief injection time compared with the lifetime τ_p, we have

$$L_1 \ll \sqrt{D_p \tau_p} \qquad (313.17)$$

and, with very large initial voltage $V(0)$, we have

$$L_1 \gg \sqrt{D_p \tau_p} \qquad (313.18)$$

(IV) Since there is an open circuit, no IR drop appears in series with the barrier, and it is assumed that the energy bands are horizontal, except within the barrier, as shown in Fig. 31.6. Therefore, the current density of holes consists entirely of the contribution by diffusion and is given by the expression

$$J_p = -qD_p \frac{\partial p_1}{\partial x}, \qquad x = w \qquad (313.19)$$

in which $\partial p_1/\partial x$ is given by the solution of the continuity equation

$$\frac{\partial p_1}{\partial t} = D_p \frac{\partial^2 p_1}{\partial x^2} - \frac{p_1}{\tau_p} \qquad (313.20)$$

subject to the boundary conditions (313.13), (313.15), and (313.16).

If one considers this boundary value problem in terms of Laplace transforms, one may obtain the following expression for $J_p'(s)$ the Laplace transform of the current density of holes at $x = w$:

$$J_p'(s) = qp_0\sqrt{D_p}\left\{\frac{-\Xi(0)}{\sqrt{s + (1/\tau_p)} + (\sqrt{D_p}/L_1)}\right.$$

$$\left. + \Xi'(s)\sqrt{s + (1/\tau_p)}\right\} \quad (313.21)$$

in which the Laplace transform of $\Xi(t)$ has been denoted by $\Xi'(s)$. It is convenient to rewrite (313.21) as follows:

$$J_p'(s) = \gamma J_s\left\{\frac{-\sqrt{\tau_p}\Xi(0)}{\sqrt{s + (1/\tau_p)} + (\sqrt{D_p}/L_1)}\right.$$

$$\left. + \Xi'(s)\sqrt{1 + s\tau_p}\right\} \quad (313.22)$$

with γ as defined by (312.10) and J_s the total saturation current density.

It follows from (I) that the diffusion length of electrons is so short in the p-type region left of the barrier (Fig. 31.6) that the electron current is essentially frequency independent compared with the hole current. Hence, we may write the electron current density

$$J_n(t) = (1 - \gamma)J_s\Xi(t) \quad (313.23)$$

which has the Laplace transform

$$J_n'(s) = (1 - \gamma)J_s\Xi'(s) \quad (313.24)$$

The Laplace transform of the total current density is the sum of (313.22) and (313.24) and this sum must vanish as there is an open circuit. Setting the sum of (313.22) and

(313.24) equal to zero, solving for $\Xi'(s)$, and finding its inverse transform, one obtains the following solution:

$$\Xi(t)/\Xi(0) = \frac{\exp(-t/\tau_p)}{(1 - \gamma) L_1 - \gamma\sqrt{D_p\tau_p}}$$

$$\times \left\{ (1 - \gamma) L_1 \exp\left[\left(\frac{1 - \gamma}{\gamma}\right)^2 \frac{t}{\tau_p}\right] \mathrm{erfc}\, \frac{1 - \gamma}{\gamma}\sqrt{\frac{t}{\tau_p}} \right.$$

$$\left. - \gamma\sqrt{D_p\tau_p} \exp \frac{D_p t}{L_1^2} \mathrm{erfc}\, \frac{\sqrt{D_p t}}{L_1} \right\} \quad (313.25)$$

With unity injection ratio ($\gamma = 1$), the solution (313.25) reduces to

$$\frac{\Xi(t)}{\Xi(0)} = \exp \left[\left(\frac{D_p\tau_p}{L_1^2} - 1\right)\frac{t}{\tau_p}\right] \mathrm{erfc}\, \frac{\sqrt{D_p t}}{L_1} \quad (313.26)$$

With $\gamma = 1$ and $L_1 = \sqrt{D_p\tau_p}$, the recovery voltage is given by the following expression, which was obtained by North and published in a paper by Lederhandler and Giacoletto (1955):

$$\frac{\Xi(t)}{\Xi(0)} = \mathrm{erfc}\, \sqrt{\frac{t}{\tau_p}} \quad (313.27)$$

However, with a much greater initial charge on the barrier capacitance, $L_1 \gg \sqrt{D_p\tau_p}$ and $\gamma = 1$, the recovery voltage is given by the following expression which was derived by Fan and quoted by the author (1953, 1955):

$$\frac{\Xi(t)}{\Xi(0)} = \exp -\frac{t}{\tau_p} \quad (313.28)$$

Because of the condition $L_1 \gg \sqrt{D_p\tau_p}$, the voltage $V(t)$ is large compared with $\kappa T/q$ for most of the recovery time, and during this time (313.28) reduces to

$$V(t) = V(0) - \kappa T t (q\tau_p)^{-1} \quad (313.29)$$

Relation (313.29) has been commonly used for the estimation of lifetime τ_p from oscilloscope readings of the linear decay of voltage with time (Curtis and Gossick, 1956).

If $\gamma = 1$ and the injection time is brief compared with the lifetime τ_p making $L_1 \ll \sqrt{D_p \tau_p}$, then (313.26) reduces to

$$\frac{\Xi(t)}{\Xi(0)} = \exp(D_p t / L_1{}^2)\ \mathrm{erfc}\ \sqrt{D_p t}/L_1 \qquad (313.30)$$

The general relation (313.25) and special case (313.29) taken together suggest an experimental method for quickly indicating whether or not the injection ratio approaches unity. For example, if the oscilloscope trace of the voltage does not decrease almost linearly with time following a deep injection $(L_1 \gg \sqrt{D_p \tau_p})$, then γ must be noticeably less than unity.

The general relation (313.25) also indicates that $V(t)$ can decrease from a positive maximum, pass through zero, attain a negative maximum and then vanish. The transition time t_1, separating the positive and negative ranges of $V(t)$ may be used to determine the injection ratio γ from the following transcendental relation:

$$\frac{1-\gamma}{\gamma} \exp\left[\left(\frac{1-\gamma}{\gamma}\right)^2 \frac{t_1}{\tau_p}\right] \mathrm{erfc}\ \frac{1-\gamma}{\gamma}\sqrt{\frac{t_1}{\tau_p}}$$

$$= \exp(t_1/\tau_p)\ \mathrm{erfc}\ \sqrt{\frac{t_1}{\tau_p}} \qquad (313.31)$$

which has been derived from (313.25) with $L_1 = \sqrt{D_p \tau_p}$. In order to make use of relation (313.31) to determine γ, the lifetime τ_p must be known, the injection time must be long compared with τ_p, and $V(0)$ must have substantially less magnitude than the equilibrium barrier height to make $L_1 = \sqrt{D_p \tau_p}$.

Following a large amplitude current pulse, the voltage, at the time the recovery commences, equals the equilibrium barrier height, provided that the metal contact at the bulk semiconductor is not separated by an insulating barrier as in the Bethe model. If, rather than a metal-germanium barrier, the type of metal-semiconducting oxide barrier, to which the Bethe model applies, is considered, then the voltage immediately after the injecting pulse may be considerably higher than the equilibrium barrier height. However, the voltage decays very rapidly to the equilibrium height, as the barrier capacitance discharges through a nonlinear conductance which is determined by space charge limiting, and the voltage decays thereafter more slowly as the barrier capacitance discharges through the forward conductance of a semiconducting rectifying barrier. Although the initial decay is rapid, while the final decay is slow, there is not a sharp discontinuity in the slope of the decay voltage with time, and the transition between the two modes of decay is insufficiently obvious to delineate an estimate of V_B. Typical curves of the recovery voltage as a function of time are shown in Fig. 31.7 for a germanium rectifier, and in Fig. 31.8 for a ceramic rutile diode.

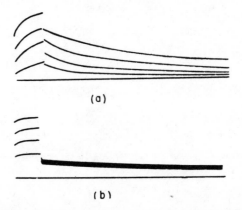

(a)

(b)

Fig. 31.7. Terminal voltage across a germanium p-n junction against time with varying amounts of current injection. (a) Curves obtained with low amplitude pulses. (b) Curves showing the saturation of the post-injection emf obtained with large current pulses. [From Gossick (1955).]

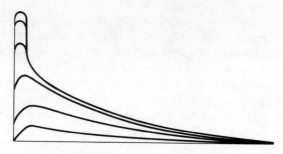

Fig. 31.8. Terminal voltage across a gold-ceramic rutile barrier against time with varying amounts of current injection.

Exercises

(3.12) Starting from (312.9), derive (313.6) for a planar barrier, in which minority carriers dominate the total current.

(3.13) Extend the derivation of (313.25) to apply to a hemispherical junction of radius r_2, defining the boundary of the space charge region corresponding to $x = w$ in the planar case, and show that the solution is the same as (313.25) with γ replaced by $\gamma r_2 (\sqrt{D_p \tau_p} + r_2)^{-1}$.

List of Symbols

a	Lattice spacing
b	Reciprocal length (311.8)
c_1	Velocity of light in vacuum
c_s	Velocity of sound in metal
d	Reciprocal length (311.7)
e	Base of Naperian logarithms
f_0	Fermi distribution function
f_1	Amplitude by which the Fermi distribution function is perturbed by an ac field
f_s	Modified Fermi distribution function (112.4)
$g(E)$	Density of energy states
g_s	Density of energy states of the s group of electrons
h	Planck's constant
$\hbar$	Planck's constant multiplied by $(2\pi)^{-1}$
i	$\sqrt{-1}$
j	An integer
$\mathbf{k}, \mathbf{k}'$	Wave vector
k_1, k_2, k_3	Cartesian components of $\mathbf{k}$
k_r, k_i	Real and imaginary components of the wave vector along a particular axis
k_δ	Small variation in k from that which gives either a minimum or maximum in electron energy
l	An integer
m	Electronic mass
m^*, m_h^*, m_m^*	Effective mass of an electron and hole in a semiconductor and a "hot" electron in a metal

$\left(\dfrac{m}{m^*}\right)_{ij}$ Normalized element of the reciprocal mass tensor

n Density of electrons

n_i Density of electrons for the intrinsic temperature range

n_0 Electron density parameter (103.11); taking the potential as zero where the carrier concentrations have equilibrium values, n_0 becomes the equilibrium concentration

n_n, n_p Concentration of conduction electrons on the n side and p side of a p-n junction

n_{p0} Equilibrium value of n_p

n_s Density of electrons in the s group

$\langle nv_1 \rangle$ Mean electron flux in the x_1 direction

n Principal quantum number

$\mathbf{p}$ Momentum

p_1, p_2, p_3 Cartesian components of $\mathbf{p}$

p Density of holes

p_0 Equilibrium value of p

p_1 Excess hole concentration ($p - p_0$)

p_n, p_p Concentration of holes on the n side and p side of a p-n junction

p_{n0} Equilibrium value of p_n

q Electronic charge

r Radial coordinate

r_1, r_2 Radii defining the inner and outer boundaries of a hemispherical metal-semiconductor barrier

r_B Bohr radius, 0.529 Å

r_{dn}, r_{an} Orbital radius of electron bound to a donor impurity, (101.56), and of a hole bound to an acceptor impurity, (101.58), according to the hydrogenic model

r_{si} Coordinate in a lattice

s An integer

t Time

u	Energy density
$\mathbf{v(k)}$	Velocity associated with the wave vector $\mathbf{k}$
$v_1,\ v_2,\ v_3$	Cartesian components of $\mathbf{v}$
$\langle v \rangle$	Mean drift velocity of electrons
v_{diff}	Diffusion velocity (125.15)
$\mathbf{v}_i$	Velocity of the ith electron with respect to the centroid of a particular group of electrons
v_n	Mean thermal velocity of electrons
w	Width of a potential barrier
$x_1,\ x_2,\ x_3$	Cartesian coordinates
$x_n,\ x_p$	Boundaries of a planar p-n junction (see Fig. 21.1)
$y(x)$	Periodic function of x with period a
z	An integer
$A,\ B$	Constants of integration (311.9)
C_k	Fourier coefficient associated with the wave vector $\mathbf{k}$
C_B	Barrier capacitance
C_s	Barrier capacitance per unit area
D_m	Diffusion coefficient of hot electrons in a metal
$D_n,\ D_p$	Diffusion coefficient of electrons and holes
$\mathbf{E}$	Electric field
E_0	Electric field at the interface of a metal-semiconductor rectifying contact (the tangential component of the electric field vanishes)
E	Electron energy
E_a	Energy parameter (101.36)
E_A	Energy of an acceptor level
E_c	Lowest energy in the conduction band
E_D	Energy of a donor level
E_h	Threshold value for the initial energy of a "hot" electron
E_l	Threshold energy above which electrons are "hot"
E_R	The Rydberg, 13.6 eV

E_s	Energy of an electron in the s group
E_v	Highest energy in the valence band
E_w	Width of an electron energy band
G	Generation rate of electron-hole pairs
I	Current of charge carriers
$\mathbf{J}, J$	Current density of charge carriers
$\mathbf{J}_1, J_1$	Drift current density
$\mathbf{J}_2, J_2$	Diffusion current density
J_n, J_p	Current density of electrons and holes
J_{ns}, J_{ps}	Minority carrier saturation current density, for electrons (300.1), for holes (300.2), (302.3a)
J_{ms}	Saturation current density for electrons in a "thin" metal-semiconductor barrier (301.10)
$K_1(T), K_2(T),$ $K_3(T)$	Equilibrium constants used with the law of mass action, (102.12), (102.19), (102.24)
L_c	A characteristic length (104.5)
L_D	Debye length (211.3)
L_m	Attenuation length of "hot" electrons in a metal $L_m = \sqrt{D_m \tau_m}$
L_m'	ac Value of L_m, e.g., $L_m/\sqrt{1 + i\omega\tau_m}$
L_n, L_p	Diffusion length of electrons and holes
L_p'	ac Value of L_p, e.g., $L_p/\sqrt{1 + i\omega\tau_p}$
L_0	Length of a semiconducting sample
N	A very large even number
N_A	Density of neutral acceptor impurities
N_{A-}	Density of ionized acceptor impurities
$N_A{}^0$	Sum of N_A and N_{A-}
N_c	Effective density of states in the conduction band
N_D	Density of neutral donor impurities
N_{D+}	Density of ionized donor impurities
$N_D{}^0$	Sum of N_D and N_{D+}
N_v	Effective density of states in the valence band
N_τ	Density of recombination centers

$P(w)$	Dimensionless parameter (311.15)
Q	Charge
$Q_s(V)$	Charge per unit area of the barrier double layer as a function of bias voltage V
R	Electrical resistance
S	Entropy
T	Absolute temperature
V	Voltage applied across a potential barrier
V'	Amplitude of a small ac perturbation on the bias V
V_B	Equilibrium barrier height
W	Number of distinguishable distributions of an electron gas (111.1), (112.3)
$Y(i\omega)$	Barrier admittance (311.16), (312.9), (312.11), (313.5)
α	The fine structure constant $(137)^{-1}$
$\alpha_1, \beta_1, \gamma_1$	Lagrangian multipliers (112.4)
γ	Injection ratio (312.10)
δ	Thickness of the insulating layer separating the metal from the semiconductor in the Bethe model
ϵ	Permittivity
ζ	Fermi level
$\zeta_i(x)$	Intrinsic Fermi level, serving as the potential energy of an electron
ζ_n, ζ_p	Electrochemical potentials (quasi-Fermi levels) of electrons and holes
ζ_1	Small perturbation on ζ, (114.2)
η	Energy parameter equal to $E + \zeta_i/2 - 2E_a$
θ_n	Number of energy minima in the conduction band over the reduced zone
θ_p	Number of energy maxima in the valence band over the reduced zone
κ	Boltzmann's constant
λ	Electronic mean free path
λ_m	Mean free path of "hot" electrons in a metal

$\lambda_{me}, \lambda_{mf}$	Mean free path of "hot" electrons in a metal, from electron-electron and from electron-phonon interactions
λ_n	Mean free path of conduction electrons in a semiconductor
μ_n, μ_p	Mobility of electrons and holes in a semiconductor
ν	Mean number of collisions required to convert a hot electron to a cool electron
ξ	A constant defined by (313.7)
$\sigma, \sigma_1, \sigma_2, \sigma_3$	Designations of an integer
$\sigma(x)$	Instantaneous conductivity equal to $q[\mu_n n(x) + \mu_p p(x)]$
σ_0	Equilibrium value of conductivity
σ_n	Conductivity by electrons
τ	Collision time of electrons
τ_m	Attenuation time of hot electrons in a metal
τ_n, τ_p	Electron-hole recombination time in p-type and n-type material, respectively
τ_s	Collision time of electrons in the s group
φ	Fermi level, according to the relation $-q\varphi = \zeta$
φ_n, φ_p	Electrochemical potentials (quasi-Fermi levels) of electrons and holes, respectively, according to the relations $-q\varphi_n = \zeta_n$ and $-q\varphi_p = \zeta_p$
$\varphi_i(x)$	Potential function satisfying the relation $-q\varphi_i(x) = \zeta_i(x)$ with $\zeta_i(x)$ the potential energy of an electron
χ	A constant defined by (313.8)
$\psi(x)$	Electronic wave function
ω	Angular frequency
$\Gamma(x)$	Amplitude of the ac component of $\exp[\zeta_n(x) - \zeta]/\kappa T$

Δ	Energy separation between band edge and localized state
Δ_{dn}	Energy separation between conduction band edge and donor level with principal quantum number n, i.e., $(E_D - E_c)$
Δ_{an}	Energy separation between valence band edge and acceptor level with principal quantum number n, i.e., $(E_v - E_A)$
Θ	Barrier charging time constant,

$$C_B\left(\frac{dI}{dV}\right)_{dc}^{-1}$$

$\Lambda(x)$	Exponent of the modified Fermi distribution function (112.5a), (112.6), (114.3)
$\Xi(t)$	$[\exp(qV(t)/\kappa T)] - 1$
Σ	Cross section of recombination centers
Υ	Electron-hole recombination rate
Φ	Heat flux
$\Psi(\eta)$	A function of electron energy (101.53)
$\Omega(V)$	Number of occupied boundary states per unit area, as a function of bias voltage

APPENDIX B

Properties of Semiconductors

Material	Band gap (eV)	Reference
Si	1.15	(Fan and Becker, 1951)
Ge	0.76	(Fan and Becker, 1951)
GaAs	1.4	(Edwards *et al.*, 1959)
PbS	0.37	(Scanlon, 1959)
TiO_2 (rutile)	3.05	(Cronemeyer, 1952)

All values listed correspond to room temperature.

Electron mobility $(cm)^2(volt\ sec)^{-1}$	Hole mobility $(cm)^2(volt\ sec)^{-1}$	Reference
1200	250	(Haynes and Westphal, 1952)
3800	1800	(Prince, 1953)
4000	400	(Aukerman *et al.*, 1963)
~800	~1000	(Scanlon, 1959)
1.0 *c* direction 0.2 *a* direction	—	(Frederikse, 1961)

APPENDIX C

Difference Equation Approximation of the Laplacian

Consider the Taylor expansion of a function $f(\mathbf{r})$ about a point in a Cartesian system, to the second order:

$$f(\mathbf{r}) = f(\mathbf{r}_1) + \left(\frac{\partial f}{\partial x}\right)_{r_1} dx + \left(\frac{\partial f}{\partial y}\right)_{r_1} dy + \left(\frac{\partial f}{\partial z}\right)_{r_1} dz$$

$$+ \frac{1}{2}\left(\frac{\partial^2 f}{\partial x^2}\right)_{r_1} (dx)^2 + \frac{1}{2}\left(\frac{\partial^2 f}{\partial y^2}\right)_{r_1} (dy)^2 + \frac{1}{2}\left(\frac{\partial^2 f}{\partial z^2}\right)_{r_1} (dz)^2$$

$$+ \left(\frac{\partial^2 f}{\partial x\,\partial y}\right)_{r_1} dx\,dy + \left(\frac{\partial^2 f}{\partial x\,\partial z}\right)_{r_1} dx\,dz$$

$$+ \left(\frac{\partial^2 f}{\partial y\,\partial z}\right)_{r_1} dy\,dz \tag{1}$$

Let us now evaluate that function at the point 0 (x, y, z), point 1 $(x + a, y, z)$, etc., as listed in Table I.

TABLE I

Designation of point	Coordinates of point
0	(x, y, z)
1	$(x + a, y, z)$
2	$(x - a, y, z)$
3	$(x, y + a, z)$
4	$(x, y - a, z)$
5	$(x, y, z + a)$
6	$(x, y, z - a)$

The function $f_i(x,\ y,\ z)$ is given to the second order at each point $(i = 1, 2, 3, 4, 5, 6)$ by the following relations:

$$f_1 = f_0 + \left(\frac{\partial f}{\partial x}\right)_0 a + \frac{1}{2}\left(\frac{\partial^2 f}{\partial x^2}\right)_0 a^2 \qquad (2)$$

$$f_2 = f_0 - \left(\frac{\partial f}{\partial x}\right)_0 a + \frac{1}{2}\left(\frac{\partial^2 f}{\partial x^2}\right)_0 a^2 \qquad (3)$$

$$f_3 = f_0 + \left(\frac{\partial f}{\partial y}\right)_0 a + \frac{1}{2}\left(\frac{\partial^2 f}{\partial y^2}\right)_0 a^2 \qquad (4)$$

$$f_4 = f_0 - \left(\frac{\partial f}{\partial y}\right)_0 a + \frac{1}{2}\left(\frac{\partial^2 f}{\partial y^2}\right)_0 a^2 \qquad (5)$$

$$f_5 = f_0 + \left(\frac{\partial f}{\partial z}\right)_0 a + \frac{1}{2}\left(\frac{\partial^2 f}{\partial z^2}\right)_0 a^2 \qquad (6)$$

$$f_6 = f_0 - \left(\frac{\partial f}{\partial z}\right)_0 a + \frac{1}{2}\left(\frac{\partial^2 f}{\partial z^2}\right)_0 a^2 \qquad (7)$$

One may add (2) through (7) to obtain the following difference equation approximation of the Laplacian:

$$\left(\frac{\partial^2 f}{\partial x^2}\right)_0 + \left(\frac{\partial^2 f}{\partial y^2}\right)_0 + \left(\frac{\partial^2 f}{\partial z^2}\right)_0$$

$$= \frac{f_1 + f_2 + f_3 + f_4 + f_5 + f_6 - 6f_0}{a^2} \qquad (8)$$

If the function $f(\mathbf{r})$ has just one variable x, then one merely adds (2) and (3) to obtain the one-dimensional Laplacian

$$\left(\frac{d^2 f}{dx^2}\right)_0 = \frac{f_1 + f_2 - 2f_0}{a^2} \qquad (9)$$

REFERENCES

ARMSTRONG, H. L. (1956). *J. Appl. Phys.* **27**, 420.

AUKERMAN, L. W., DAVIS, P. W., GRAFT, R. D., and SHILLIDAY, T. S. (1963). *J. Appl. Phys.* **34**, 3590.

BARDEEN, J., and MORRISON, S. R. (1954). *Physica* **20**, 873.

BARSUKOV, IN. K. (1957). *Soviet Phys.—Tech. Phys.* **2**, 2094.

BECKER, M., and FAN, H. Y. (1950). *Phys. Rev.* **78**, 301.

BETHE, H. A. (1942). "Theory of the Boundary Layer of Crystal Rectifiers." *Mass. Inst. Technol. Rept.* 43–12.

BLAKEMORE, J. (1962). "Semiconductor Statistics." Pergamon Press, London and New York.

BOHM, D., and PINES, D. (1953). *Phys. Rev.* **92**, 609.

BRAY, R. (1949). Ph.D. Thesis, Purdue University.

BRAY, R., and GOSSICK, B. (1953). *Phys. Rev.* **91**, 1011.

BRILLOUIN, L. (1934). *Helv. Phys. Acta Suppl.* **2**, 47.

BROOKS, H. (1955). *Advan. Electron. Electron Phys.* **7**, 85.

CALLAWAY, J. (1958). *Solid State Phys.* **7**.

CALLAWAY, J. (1964). "Energy Band Theory." Academic Press, New York.

CHYNOWETH, A. G. (1960). *In* "Progress in Semiconductors" (A. F. Gibson, F. A. Kroger, and R. E. Burgess, eds.), Vol. 4. Wiley, New York.

CRAWFORD, J. H., and HOLMES, D. K. (1954). *Proc. Phys. Soc.* **A67**, 294.

CRONEMEYER, D. C. (1952). *Phys. Rev.* **87**, 876.

CURTIS, O., and GOSSICK, B. (1956). *IRE Trans. Electron Devices* **3**, 163.

DEMBER, H. (1931). *Physik. Z.* **32**, 554.

EDWARDS, A. L., SLYKHOUSE, T. E., and DRICKAMER, H. G. (1959). *Phys. Chem. Solids* **11**, 140.

ENGLER, H. D. (1960). *Nukleonik* **2**, 215.

ENGLISH, F., and GOSSICK, B. (1964). *Solid-State Electron.* **7**, 193.

ESAKI, L. (1958). *Phys. Rev.* **109**, 603.

FAN, H. Y., and BECKER, M. (1951). *In* "Semiconducting Materials" (H. K. Henisch, ed.). Academic Press, New York.

FOWLER, R. H. (1933). *Proc. Roy. Soc.* **A140**, 505.

FREDERIKSE, H. P. R. (1961). *J. Appl. Phys. Suppl.* **32**, 2211.

FRENKEL, J. and JOFFE, A. (1932). *Physik. Z. Sowjetunion* **1**, 60.

FRITZSCHE, H., and LARK-HOROVITZ, K. (1954). *Physica* **20**, 834.

GOSSICK, B. R. (1953). *Phys. Rev.* **91**, 1012.

GOSSICK, B. R. (1955). *J. Appl. Phys.* **26**, 1356; *Proc. Natl. Electron. Conf.* **11**, 602.

GOSSICK, B. R. (1956). *J. Appl. Phys.* **27**, 905.

GOSSICK, B. R. (1960). *J. Appl. Phys.* **31**, 29.

GOSSICK, B. R. (1963). *Solid-State Electron.* **6**, 445.

GOUCHER, F. S., PEARSON, G. L., SPARKS, M., TEAL, G. K., and SHOCK-LEY, W., (1951). *Phys. Rev.* **81**, 637.

HAGSTRUM, H. D. (1959). *Phys. Chem. Solids* **8**, 211.

HAYNES, J. R., and WESTPHAL, W. C. (1952). *Phys. Rev.* **85**, 680.

HENISCH, H. K. (1957). "Rectifying Semi-conductor Contacts." Oxford Univ. Press, London and New York.

HERMAN, F. (1955). *Proc. I.R.E. (Inst. Radio Engrs.)* **43**, 1703.

HERMAN, F. (1958). *Rev. Mod. Phys.* **30**, 102.

HUNG, C. S. (1950). *Phys. Rev.* **79**, 727.

JAMES, H. M. (1949). *Phys. Rev.* **76**, 1602.

JAMES, H. M., and WEISS, P. R. (1947). "Theory of Servomechanisms." McGraw-Hill, New York.

KANAI, Y. (1954). *J. Phys. Soc. Japan* **9**, 143.

KANAI, Y. (1955). *J. Phys. Soc. Japan* **10**, 719.

Ko, W.-H. (1961). *Solid-State Electron.* **3**, 59.

KOENIG, S. H. (1959). *Phys. Chem. Solids* **8**, 227.

KOHN, W. (1959). *Phys. Chem. Solids* **8**, 45.

KRON, G. (1945). *Phys. Rev.* **67**, 39.

LAMPERT, M. A. (1959). *RCA Rev.* **20**, 682.

LAMPERT, M. A. (1961). *Proc. Intern. Conf. Semicond. Phys. Prague, 1960* p. 232.

LAMPERT, M. A. (1962). *Proc. I.R.E. (Inst. Radio Engrs.)* **50**, 1781.

LAX, B., and NEUSTADTER, S. F. (1954). *J. Appl. Phys.* **25**, 1148.

LEDERHANDLER, S. R., and GIACOLETTO, L. J. (1955). *Proc. I.R.E. (Inst. Radio Engrs.)* **43**, 447.

LINDMAYER, J., and SLOBODSKOY, A. (1963). *Solid-State Electron.* **6**, 495.

MAYER, J. W. (1959). *J. Appl. Phys.* **30**, 1937.

MOTT, N. F. (1939). *Proc. Roy. Soc.* **A117**, 27.

MOTT, N. F., and GURNEY, R. W. (1948). "Electronic Processes in Ionic Crystals" 2nd ed. Oxford Univ. Press, London and New York.

NORDHEIM, L. (1932). *Z. Physik* **75**, 434.

PELL, E. M. (1953). *Phys. Rev.* **90**, 278.

PINES, D., and BOHM, D. (1952). *Phys. Rev.* **85**, 338.

PRINCE, M. B. (1953). *Phys. Rev.* **92**, 681.

RATH, H. L. (1956). *Nachrtechber.* **5**, 15.

SABY, J. S. (1956). *Rept. Phys. Soc. Meeting Semicond. Rugby, U.K.* p. 39.

SCANLON, W. W. (1959). *Solid State Phys.* **9**, 83.

SCHOTTKY, W. (1939). *Z. Physik.* **113**, 367.

SCHOTTKY, W. (1942). *Z. Physik* **118**, 539.

SCHULTZ, W. (1954). *Z. Physik* **138**, 598.

SCHWARZ, R., and WALSH, J. (1953). *Proc. I.R.E. (Inst. Radio Engrs.)* **41**, 1715.

SHOCKLEY, W. (1949). *Bell System Tech. J.* **28**, 435.

SHOCKLEY, W. (1950). "Electrons and Holes in Semiconductors." Van Nostrand, Princeton, New Jersey.

SHOCKLEY, W. (1961). *Solid-State Electron.* **2**, 35.

SHOTOV, A. P. (1958). *Soviet Phys.—Tech. Phys.* **3**, 413.

SHULMAN, R. G., and MCMAHON, M. E. (1953). *J. Appl. Phys.* **24**, 1267.

SLATER, J. C. (1949). *Phys. Rev.* **76**, 1592.

SPENKE, E. (1958). *Z. Angew. Phys.* **10**, 65.

STEELE, E. (1954). *J. Appl. Phys.* **25**, 916.

STUBBE, L., and GOSSICK, B. (1958). *J. Appl. Phys.* **30**, 507.

SWANSON, J. A. (1954). *J. Appl. Phys.* **25**, 314.

TAMM, I. (1932). *Phys. Z. Sowjetunion* **1**, 733.

TAUC, J. (1962). "Photo and Thermoelectric Effects in Semiconductors." Pergamon Press, London and New York.

TOMBOULIAN, D. H., and BEDO, D. E. (1956). *Phys. Rev.* **104**, 590.

TORREY, H. C., and WHITMER, C. A. (1948). "Crystal Rectifiers." McGraw-Hill, New York.

VAN ROOSBROECK, W. (1950). *Bell System Tech. J.* **29**, 560.

VUL, B. M., and SEGAL, B. I. (1958). *Soviet Phys.—Tech. Phys.* **3**, 638.

WAGNER, C. (1931). *Physik. Z.* **32**, 641.

WALTZ, M. C. (1952). *Proc. I.R.E. (Inst. Radio Engrs.)* **40**, 1483.

WANNIER, G. H. (1959). "Elements of Solid State Theory." Cambridge Univ. Press, London and New York.

WILSON, A. H. (1932). *Proc. Roy. Soc.* **A136**, 487.

YEARIAN, H. (1948). Work summarized by Torrey and Whitmer (1948).

SUBJECT INDEX